ARRANGIN(

How To Books on business and management

Arranging Insurance	Managing Yourself
Be a Freelance Sales Agent	Market Yourself
Buy & Run a Shop	Master Book-Keeping
Buy & Run a Small Hotel	Master Public Speaking
Cash From Your Computer	Mastering Business English
Collecting a Debt	Organising Effective Training
Communicate at Work	Prepare a Business Plan
Conduct Staff Appraisals	Publish a Book
Conducting Effective Interviews	Publish a Newsletter
Conducting Effective Negotiations	Raise Business Finance
Doing Business Abroad	Sell Your Business
Do Your Own Advertising	Start a Business from Home
Do Your Own PR	Start Your Own Business
Employ & Manage Staff	Starting to Manage
Investing in Stocks & Shares	Successful Mail Order Marketing
Keep Business Accounts	Taking on Staff
Manage a Sales Team	Understand Finance at Work
Manage an Office	Use the Internet
Manage Computers at Work	Winning Presentations
Manage People at Work	Write a Report
Managing Budgets & Cash Flows	Write & Sell Computer Software
Managing Meetings	Writing Business Letters

Other titles in preparation

The How To series now contains more than 200 titles in the following categories:

Business Basics
Family Reference
Jobs & Careers
Living & Working Abroad
Student Handbooks
Successful Writing

Please send for a free copy of the latest catalogue for full details (see back cover for address).

BUSINESS BASICS

ARRANGING INSURANCE

How to manage policies and claims for
everyday personal and business purposes

Terry Hallett

How To Books

Cartoons by Mike Flanagan

British Library Cataloguing in Publication Data
A catalogue record for this book is available from the British Library.

© Copyright 1997 by Terry Hallett.

First published in 1997 by How To Books Ltd, 3 Newtec Place,
Magdalen Road, Oxford OX4 1RE, United Kingdom.
Tel: (01865) 793806. Fax: (01865) 248780.

Note: The material contained in this book is set out in good faith for general
guidance and no liability can be accepted for loss or expense incurred as a
result of relying in particular circumstances on statements made in the book.
The laws and regulations are complex and liable to change, and readers
should check the current position with the relevant authorities before making
personal arrangements.

Produced for How To Books by Deer Park Productions.

Typeset by Concept Communications (Design & Print) Ltd, Crayford, Kent.
Printed and bound by Cromwell Press, Broughton Gifford, Melksham, Wiltshire.

Contents

List of illustrations   8

Preface   9

1   **Choosing your insurances**   11

    Thinking positive   11
    Selecting household buildings cover   11
    Selecting household contents cover   13
    Deciding on other miscellaneous covers 17
    Insuring your vehicle   19
    Running a business from home   24
    Checklist   26
    Case studies (introduction)   30
    Discussion points   30

2   **Selecting the scope of policy covers**   32

    Thinking positive   32
    Checking cover   32
    Deciding on additional covers   38
    Assessing the sum insured   41
    Thinking about the cost   51
    Checklist   53
    Case studies   55
    Discussion points   55

3   **Taking out policies**   57

    Thinking positive   57
    Buying your insurance   57
    Completing the proposal form   61
    Dealing direct with insurance companies 63
    Using an insurance broker   64
    Using an agent/consultant   64
    Receiving and renewing your policy   65
    Checklist   66
    Case studies   67
    Discussion points   68

4   **Taking action after a loss**   69

     Thinking positive   69
     Checking your policy cover   69
     Notifying your insurers   71
     Dealing with advisors   73
     Understanding the role of broker/consultant   75
     Checklist   75
     Case studies   76
     Discussion points   78

5   **Compiling your claim**   79

     Thinking positive   79
     Assessing your claim   80
     Obtaining repair/replacement costs   81
     Dealing with professional advisors   83
     Completing the claim form   90
     Planning and acting   92
     Checklist   94
     Case studies   94
     Discussion points   96

6   **Submitting your claim**   97

     Thinking positive   97
     Organising the presentation   97
     Timing the submission of details   98
     Heading-off queries   99
     Keeping the claim moving   101
     Checklist   102
     Case studies   103
     Discussion points   105

7   **Dealing with your insurance company**   106

     Thinking positive   106
     Recording contacts   106
     Confirming discussions and actions   108
     Addressing problems   108
     Preventing delays   110
     Arranging payments under policy   112
     Checklist   113
     Case studies   113
     Discussion points   115

8   **Negotiating a settlement**   116

     Thinking positive   116
     Agreeing the basis of settlement   116
     Dealing with offers   125

Arranging claim payments   126
Knowing your rights concerning payment   127
Checklist   128
Case studies   129
Discussion points   131

9   **Handling disputes**   132

Thinking positive   132
Disputing policy liability   132
Disputing settlement amount   134
Pursuing your case   137
Using the Insurance Ombudsman   138
Checklist   139
Case studies   140
Discussion points   142

10 **Concluding claim settlement**   143

Thinking positive   143
Signing discharge forms   143
Paying the claim   146
Receiving *ex gratia* payments   147
Knowing the position on tax and duty   148
Recovering money from a third party   148
Dealing with salvage   149
Checklist   149
Case studies   150
Discussion points   152

11 **Insuring for the future**   153

Thinking positive   153
Penalising claims   153
Changing insurance companies   155
Valuing your property after a loss   156
Adapting to a changing market   157
Checklist   159
Case studies   160
Discussion points   160

Glossary   163

Useful addresses   167

Further reading   169

Index   171

List of Illustrations

1. Definitions page from a motor policy   20
2. Specimen certificate of motor insurance   22
3. Typical cover provided by a business money policy   28
4. House rebuilding tables (supplied by ABI)   42
5. Checklist for house contents valuation   46
6. Definitions page from a business policy   48
7. Typical business interruption cover wording   52
8. Extract from typical household proposal form   60
9. Extract from a helpline form   84
10. Typical household claim form   86
11. Extract from motor claim form – accident details and
    declaration   88
12. A household policy claim settlement wording,
    incorporating 'average' clause   117
13. Common basis of claim settlement policy wording (contents)   119
14. Typical business policy provisions for reinstatement-as-new
    settlement   123
15. Letter to insurer disputing settlement offer   135
16. Specimen discharge form for a motor claim   145

Preface

At some stage in life, we are faced with having to buy insurance. But do we always know what we are getting in return for our hard-earned money?

If spending that same money, on some other product or service, we would probably examine every detail of the transaction. However, when buying insurance, we rarely bother to check details of our purchase. 'Too complicated' or 'can't understand all the jargon' are the usual reasons given.

The purpose of this book is to offer straightforward guidance through the complex world of insurance, and to break down some of the barriers that surround the subject.

It is impossible to provide all the answers, but by the time the last page has been read, hopefully, your understanding and grasp of insurance will have improved, so that you are better equipped to make your future insurance arrangements.

In view of the numerous types of insurance available, it is necessary to concentrate on those which most people are likely to buy, although the same principles apply to the majority of insurances. The three specific types covered in this book are:

1. Household insurances.

2. Motor insurance.

3. Insurances for a small business run from home.

The author thanks the following for their help and co-operation in producing this book: Greer, for her constant encouragement and word processing skills; Association of British Insurers; The Insurance Ombudsman Bureau; Sun Alliance Connections; General Accident Fire and Life Assurance Corporation plc; Royal Insurance plc; The Chartered Institute of Arbitrators/Personal Insurance; Arbitration Service (PIAS); British Insurance and Investment Brokers' Association (BIIBA); Insurance Brokers Registration Council.

Terry Hallett

IS THIS YOU?

Householder   Motorist

Accountant

Landlord   Tenant

Sales representative

Surveyor   Home business owner

Writer

Motorcyclist   Photographer

Solicitor

Animal/pet owner   Van driver

Musician

Artist   Publisher

Retailer

Charity worker   Management consultant

Architect

Telesalesperson   PR consultant

Employer

Freelancer   Caterer

Club official

Designer   Journalist

Business manager

Business analyst   Taxi driver

Builder

Plumber   Decorator

Market researcher

Coach driver   Event organiser

Clerical worker

Banker   Building society worker

Engineer

Voluntary worker   Health visitor

1
Choosing Your Insurances

THINKING POSITIVE

Faced with the prospect of taking out an insurance policy, many people can't be bothered to read all the small print. Their aim is to buy the cheapest policy available, irrespective of whether it is the right one to meet their needs. Few bother to examine the contract in any detail.

The test of any insurance policy is when a claim arises. Usually, it is only at that stage, when a policy is pulled out from the back of a drawer and looked at with any interest. Unfortunately, numerous policyholders then discover, too late, that their insurance cover is inappropriate or inadequate.

If you are to avoid falling into this same trap, a **positive attitude** towards insurance has to be adopted from the start, before you even buy your policy, not when you make that first claim.

SELECTING HOUSEHOLD BUILDINGS COVER

If you own your home, or pay rent under a tenancy agreement which makes you responsible for the structure, you should have **buildings' insurance cover**.

For most of us, our home is our most valuable possession, and we cannot afford to leave it unprotected. Insurance does not stop accidents happening, but when they do occur, compensation paid for the loss enables us to restore the damage.

Mortgage contract

Anyone with a building society (or bank) mortgage must insure the buildings as part of the **mortgage contract**. Usually the society arranges this insurance. They will suggest three or more insurance companies from which you can choose a policy. The selected company will pay commission to the building society.

Although it may not be drawn to your attention, you are free to nominate *any insurance company* you wish to insure your property. Of course,

11

your selection has to meet with the building society's approval but this should not be a problem if it is one of the well-known companies.

Block policies

Building societies, who arrange insurance for hundreds of thousands of properties, operate a **block policy** system. One master insurance policy insures a large number of buildings, which are listed in a schedule maintained by the society.

No individual policies are issued, but the building society borrower should be given full details of the cover provided.

What are buildings?

In an insurance policy **buildings** are defined in detail. A typical definition is:

● 'Private dwelling which is brick, stone or concrete built, roofed with slate, tiles, concrete, asphalt, metal or sheets or slabs, composed entirely of incombustible mineral ingredients.'

Also included in the definition are:

● all the *domestic* offices, stables, garages and outbuildings which are part of the property

● walls, gates and fences on or around the property.

Added to this basic description, you will normally find a list of other included elements, such as permanently installed swimming pools, tennis courts, terraces, patios, drives, paths, and fixtures and fittings.

Elements not mentioned

Although not specifically mentioned, buildings usually incorporate the following:

● foundations
● fixed central heating systems
● sanitary fittings
● fitted kitchen and bedroom units
● loft insulation
● external and internal decorations.

Warning notes

Terms of individual policies issued by different insurance companies vary.

Never assume a particular policy will include every item covered by a previous policy – or even the items listed above.

If you are in any doubt whether part of your property comes within the **buildings definition**, seek clarification from the insurance company.

Should your buildings not conform to the stated definition in the policy (for instance, if they are built of timber or roofed in thatch), notify insurers immediately. Your policy will need an endorsement stating the non-standard construction, which will probably mean a higher premium to allow for the increased risk.

A household buildings policy is intended to cover *residential* (domestic) buildings only. Any *business* activity, even the storage of your own tools and equipment used for work away from the home (such as those of a decorator or plumber), should be declared to insurers.

The selection decision

When selecting household buildings insurance, these factors need to be considered:

● What is the precise extent of the property to be insured?

● Are the buildings to be insured separately, or as part of a wider package?

● If the buildings are subject to a mortgage, ensure you receive a copy of the chosen policy, or details of the block policy in which your property is included, from the mortgage lender.

● Does the scope of buildings, as defined in the policy schedule, include all the structures and additions forming your property?

SELECTING HOUSEHOLD CONTENTS COVER

You may insure the **contents** of your home separately, or as part of a package with the buildings. This package arrangement with the same insurer, has practical advantages when it comes to claiming.

The same principles apply to contents insurance as for buildings insurance, but choosing contents cover is likely to present greater problems, due to:

● the wide ranging nature of the goods to be insured
● problems in assessing values
● variations in types of policy cover available
● financial limits placed on certain items by insurers.

What are contents?

Contents are **household goods, furnishings** and **unfixed appliances, clothing** and **personal effects**. In other words, all the things you would normally expect to find in the home.

Contents are also defined in policies by their ownership. Typically, the cover applies to all possessions belonging to you, members of your family permanently living with you, and any resident domestic employees.

This is extended to include those possessions for which they are legally responsible, to the extent of their financial liability to the owner (for example, a television set rented from a rental company).

Unmarried partners living together can take out insurance in joint names, to avoid any queries over ownership when a claim arises.

Forms of policy cover

Nowadays, many insurers require you to provide a breakdown of your contents into various categories, which are subject to different premium rates to reflect the value/risk factors. Typical headings are:

● high risk items (tv, audio and video equipment, jewellery, works of art, curios and collections)

● personal effects and clothing

● sports equipment

● freezer and refrigerator contents.

This can prove a difficult exercise, even though insurers often provide guide lists of contents values.

Some insurance companies, in an effort to provide ample cover without the policyholder having to precisely value the contents, offer a generous fixed amount of cover, for example £35,000.

The number of bedrooms and/or the postcode for the dwelling are used as a basis for calculating the premium. From tables supplied by the insurance company, you can work out your own premium. This method of insurance is simpler, and becoming more widely used.

Exclusions

Careful study of the **exclusions** listed under the definition of household contents is advisable. These vary from policy to policy, although many are common to all policies.

You may consider paying additional premium to take out extra insurance to cover one or more of these items, where this is available.

Typical exclusions are:

- *motor vehicles* – caravans, trailers, boats, canoes, surfboards, sailboards, hovercraft, aircraft, gliders and their accessories. (The motor vehicles exclusion is unlikely to include pedestrian controlled motorised machines, such as garden implements or toys/models.)

- living creatures

- trees, bushes or plants (except houseplants kept permanently in the dwelling)

- interior decorations (usually insured as 'buildings')

- plans, drawings, securities, certificates or documents of any kind (except those defined as 'money')

- external satellite dish aerials and fittings

- cookers or hobs forming part of the fitted units (normally covered as 'buildings')

- property owned or used *either wholly or partly* for business purposes (a few policies now include cover for business contents)

- property *more specifically* insured by this or any other policy.

Some cautionary points

As with all other forms of insurance, never assume a policy covers everything you think it should. Always read it thoroughly, no matter how tedious this may prove. Far better to go through the procedure now, rather than when a claim arises.

Do not be swayed by short-term handouts or other 'goodies', into buying an insurance which, in the longer term, may turn out to be an expensive mistake. Concentrate on ensuring the *basic* insurance package is what you need.

For certain items included within the household contents policy, such as money and valuables, there are monetary limits applicable, often written in fairly small print. Check the stated sums are sufficient for you. If not, they can be increased by agreement with insurers, on payment of extra premium.

One *condition* applicable to most policies, which causes regular problems, relates to unoccupancy. This condition is particularly important for those policyholders who take lengthy holidays or business trips.

If you are away for up to 30 days, cover operates as normal. But if your home is insufficiently furnished for full habitation, or is unoccupied for more than 30 days, certain specified covers no longer apply. For instance, cover may not operate for the following:

● breakage of or damage to fixed glass or sanitary fixtures

● loss or damage caused by theft, or attempted theft, vandalism or acts of malicious persons

● damage due to bursting, leaking or overflowing of water tanks, pipes or apparatus

● damage caused by leakage of oil from any fixed heating installations, pipes or apparatus.

The selection decision

As with purchasing any product, it pays to shop around for your contents insurance. Although it is easier to stick with your existing insurer, and simply pay the annual renewal premium, this could prove expensive, even where you receive a **no-claims discount** off your premium.

Useful tips when making your selection decision are:

1. Have these basic questions in mind at the outset:

    (a) Which insurer can supply the type of cover you want?
    (b) In relation to your particular goods, what can be covered?
    (c) What will be excluded from cover?
    (d) What are the basic premium rates?
    (e) What will your required cover cost?
    (f) What happens if you need to make a claim?

2. Be clear as to which members of your household possess goods that are to be included. For instance, do you have an elderly relative living with you?

3. Obtain a checklist, perhaps from one of the insurance companies you have approached, and go from room to room in your home, listing your possessions. This is advisable, even where you intend to take out a policy with a seemingly ample fixed sum insured.

4. Should you feel inclined to stay with your present insurer, give some thought to the following points:

(a) Have you received a prompt and efficient response to any previous claims?

(b) Have premium increases been above or below the market trend?

(c) Have there been improvements in the policy terms or cover at no extra cost?

5. Ensure there is no overlap between your contents policy, and other policies already in force. For example, you may have separate insurance cover on certain pieces of jewellery, or electrical appliances.

6. If you are a member of a group, or professional body, such as a nurse, teacher, trade union member, or student, check whether there is a 'special insurance scheme' arranged by that group or body available to you.

DECIDING ON OTHER MISCELLANEOUS COVERS

Household buildings and contents insurance policies include as standard a number of additional contingencies, at no extra cost. Typical examples are listed under the following two headings.

Household buildings
Household buildings' insurance policies include:

● Accidental damage to fixed glass in doors, windows, skylights, fan lights and to sanitary fixtures.

● Accidental damage to underground service pipes and cables for which *you are legally responsible*.

● Loss of rent *due to you*, or the cost of reasonable alternative accommodation if your dwelling is made uninhabitable following insured damage (financial limit applies for this cost, usually 10 per cent of buildings sum insured).

● Professional and other fees (architect's, surveyor's or legal), plus cost of emergency safety works, debris clearance and complying with statutory regulations and local authority bye-laws.

● If you have agreed to sell your home, the buyer will have the benefit of the insurance until completion of the sale (provided the buildings are not insured by any other policy).

● Where you are legally liable, *as owner*, for accidents in and around your home, resulting in injury or illness to a third party or loss of or damage to property, your buildings' insurers will cover all sums payable by you.

Household contents
Household contents insurance policies include:

● **Your legal liability** for sums payable under terms of any credit, debit, charge, cheque or cash card held solely for *domestic* purposes, following its loss and fraudulent use in the UK or the rest of Europe (usually subject to a limit, typically £500).

● **Alternative accommodation costs** or loss of rent *payable by you or to you*, while your dwelling remains uninhabitable following insured loss or damage (subject to financial limit varying between 10 per cent and 20 per cent of contents sum insured).

● **Payment of fixed sum** (usually £5,000) should you or your spouse die within 30 days of suffering injury as a result of:

 – accident, assault or fire in the home
 – an accident while travelling as a fare-paying passenger by train, bus or licensed taxi
 – assault in the street.

● **Your legal liability** as a *tenant* of your home for damage to the structure and decorations (subject to limit of 10 per cent of contents sum insured).

● **Payment of irrecoverable court awards** – where your household has been awarded a sum by a UK court and this has not been paid to you within three months of the award (subject to certain specified conditions).

Extending your policy
In addition to those additional covers, included as part of the standard policy package, you may wish to extend your policy to cover other items, possibly at extra cost.

These optional extensions could include:

● insurance for replacement external door locks and keys, where the original keys have been stolen

● insurance for the contents of a domestic deep freezer, against deterioration due to breakdown, accidental damage or failure of the temperature control device

● insurance of sporting equipment against damage or theft anywhere

● insurance of pedal cycles (usually subject to an individual item limit)

● insurance for satellite receiving equipment and/or home computer equipment

● insurance of caravans or small boats, used for pleasure purposes only.

INSURING YOUR VEHICLE

Why insure?

You have to arrange insurance on your car, or other motor vehicle to be used on the road, because the law makes it compulsory, under the Road Traffic Act 1988 (revised 1991).

Apart from the legal requirement, many motorists choose to insure a vehicle, so they may be in a position to have it replaced or repaired without delay, in the event of an accident or theft.

What insurances are available?

There are three types of cover:

1. **Third party only** – this is the minimum cover required by law, and is best suited to cars of low value. It covers damage to third party vehicles or property damaged in an accident, as well as any third party injury. There is no cover for your own vehicle.

2. **Third party, fire and theft** – in addition to third party only insurance, this provides cover for fire damage and theft in respect of your own vehicle.

3. **Comprehensive** – as well as insuring 'third party' and 'fire and theft', a comprehensive policy gives cover for damage to your own vehicle. There are also additional benefits included, which vary between different policies. Benefits likely to be included are:

   – 'replacement as new' for cars under 12 months old, stolen or irreparably damaged, which have been bought new.
   – personal accident cover for you or your spouse arising from a

Definitions

The schedule

details of you and the insurance protection provided

Certificate of Motor Insurance

a certificate that proves you have the motor insurance you must have by law.
It states who can drive your car and what purposes it can be used for

International Motor Insurance Card (Green Card)

proof that you are insured to drive your car in the countries the card is for

You

the policyholder (the person named in the schedule)

Car

a motor car designed to be used on public roads

Your car

the car shown in the schedule which belongs to you, is leased by you or which
you or your wife or husband are buying under a hire purchase agreement

We/Us/Our/General Accident

General Accident Fire and Life Assurance Corporation p.l.c.

Fire

fire, lightning or explosion

Theft

theft or attempted theft

The period of insurance

the period of time covered by this policy as shown in the schedule, and any
further period we accept your premium for

Market value

the cost of replacing your car with one of similar type and condition

Territorial limits

the United Kingdom, any country in the European Community, Austria,
Czech Republic, Finland, Hungary, Norway, Slovak Republic, Sweden and
Switzerland

United Kingdom

England, Scotland, Wales, Northern Ireland, the Isle of Man and the Channel
Islands

Endorsement

changes in the terms of the policy. These are shown in your schedule

Policy excess

the amount you will have to pay if your car is lost, stolen or damaged

Fig. 1. Definitions page from a motor policy.

motor accident, resulting in death, loss of eyes or limbs (usually subject to a maximum between £3,000 and £5,000).

– payment of medical expenses for bodily injuries sustained by the driver or passengers or of insured car in accident (often limit of £150 per person).

– loss of or damage to rugs, clothing and personal effects while in insured car, resulting from fire, theft or other accidental means.

– damage to windscreens or car windows (subject to an excess, usually about £40).

On inspecting the range of comprehensive policies available, many other added benefits can be found. These could include cover for in-car audio equipment, or payment for emergency overnight accommodation. Each policy has to be analysed in relation to your specific needs.

Points to bear in mind

1. Most policies cover the policyholder while driving a vehicle belonging to another person, with that person's permission. But the cover is limited to the third party liability only. You would *not* be insured for any damage to the borrowed vehicle. Should the owner of a borrowed car have comprehensive cover on an any-driver basis, then damage to the vehicle would also be insured.

   Before driving anyone else's car, check the owner's insurance cover, rather than relying on the limited third party cover provided by your own policy.

2. Sometimes cover is deleted from a policy for driving other cars. Examples where this arises are cars insured in a company's name, a driver who has a bad driving record, or a very young inexperienced driver. In the cases of the drivers, this is to restrict them to driving the car known to insurers, and prevent the borrowing of a fast, unfamiliar model.

3. If you are covered as 'spouse' on a 'named driver and spouse only' comprehensive policy, the insurance does not cover you while driving someone else's vehicle.

   Unless the vehicle owner has an 'any-driver' policy, you would be driving unlawfully and would be personally liable for any injuries or damage caused in an accident.

4. Should you give a lift to someone who contributes to the cost of the journey, your insurance cover will not be jeopardised. There could be

SUN ALLIANCE
INSURANCE UK

MOTOR DIRECT

Certificate of Motor Insurance

B

Certificate number   33/M000191132/A003016

Code   3A8F

---

1. Registration Mark/Description of vehicle

Any motor car owned by the Policyholder or hired to her under a hire purchase or annual leasing agreement

2. Name of Policyholder

Joanne Testminu5

3. Effective date for the commencement of Insurance for the purposes of the relevant law

31 January 1995

4. Date of expiry of Insurance

29 January 1996

5. Persons or classes of persons entitled to drive

The Policyholder

The Policyholder may also drive a motor car neither belonging to her, nor hired to her under a hire purchase or annual leasing agreement

Provided that the person driving holds a licence to drive the vehicle (or has held and is not disqualified for holding or obtaining such a licence) and is driving on the Policyholder's order or with her permission.

6. Limitations as to use

Use for social domestic and pleasure purposes
Use by the Policyholder and the Policyholder's spouse in person for their businesses

The Policy does not cover
Speed testing pacemaking or competitive driving
Use for commercial travelling hire or reward

I hereby certify that the Policy to which this Certificate relates satisfies the requirements of the relevant law applicable in Great Britain, Northern Ireland, the Isle of Man, the Island of Guernsey, the Island of Jersey and the Island of Alderney.

Sun Alliance and London Insurance plc (Authorised Insurers)

Rochelle .

J Rochelle
Managing Director
Sun Alliance Insurance UK

SUN ALLIANCE
INSURANCE UK

In the event of an accident please telephone the Helpline on 0800 010144 for help and advice

Keep your Certificate in a safe place but not in your vehicle

Please note that the Driving Other Cars cover referred to in Section 5 of the Certificate of Insurance is restricted to Third Party only. Damage, fire and theft are not covered.

Note

For full details of the insurance cover reference should be made to the Policy. It is essential to notify the Insurer if you change your vehicle or acquire another

Advice to Third Parties

Nothing contained in this Certificate affects your right as a Third Party to make a claim

Duty of Disclosure

This Policy has been issued on the basis of information provided when applying for insurance and any additional details you may have given us since. Any changes which may materially affect the risk must be advised to us immediately. A list of the most common changes is shown on the back of the letter accompanying this Certificate, but it is not exhaustive. If you are in any doubt as to whether any information is material, it should be disclosed as failure to do so could invalidate the insurance. You should keep a record (including copies of letters) of all information provided.

Taking the vehicle abroad Before you depart you must apply for a Foreign Use Extension to extend your full policy cover to the continent of Europe.

Fig. 2. Specimen certificate of motor insurance.

23

a problem if you made a profit from the arrangement, as this would be construed as a business transaction.

The selection decision

Motor insurance is the source of more complaints and disputes than any other branch of the industry. Many arise over valuation of the vehicle concerned, but often problems stem from the fact the owner chose an unsuitable policy, or perhaps an inefficient insurer at the outset, guided solely by cost considerations.

Prior to shopping around for the most cost-effective deal, the first priority is to be clear on the basic insurance requirements to suit you and your vehicle. Then you can go out to seek the right policy at the right price.

Numerous choices are available, as insurers constantly amend their covers and premium rates in an effort to win a greater share of this vast market. There is always a good deal available, if you are prepared to look for it.

If you are aged over 50, or belong to an organisation or trade body that has arranged a package deal for its members, you should be able to obtain beneficial terms.

RUNNING A BUSINESS FROM HOME

Due to the cost savings on, for example, rent, rates, cost of public utilities and cleaning, an increasing number of people are working from home. The advantages are clear for anyone setting up a new small business.

A wide scope of businesses are run from home, ranging from craftsmen like furniture repairers, to professional advisers, such as accountants. Taking in paying guests or lodgers is an increasingly popular home business venture.

Assuming you have satisfied yourself there is nothing in your house deeds to prevent you operating a business from home, and the local authority have no objection, the next step is to consider the insurance implications.

Effect on household insurances

You should immediately notify your household buildings and contents insurers if you start working from home. Using the home for business, and failing to inform insurers could invalidate your household cover, even when an incident giving rise to a claim is unrelated to the business, such as a burst water pipe.

If no additional hazards are involved, like the storage of combustible materials, your household cover should remain in force.

But should people regularly call on you due to your business, you may not be insured for theft, unless there has been forcible entry or exit.

Household contents policies can rarely be extended to cover 'tools of the trade'. If you have acquired tools or other equipment at your home, they will need special insurance.

One area of insurance always affected when a business is carried out from home is legal liability for injury to third parties, or damage to their property. Household policies specifically exclude liability arising from a trade, profession or employment, so this must be insured separately with a public liability policy.

Taking in guests or lodgers

Should you take in paying guests or lodgers, you must tell your household insurers. Your policy may exclude loss or damage to any property while your home, or any part of it, is lent, let or sub-let.

It is possible your insurers will agree to endorse your policy, continuing your household insurance, but there are likely to be restrictions applied, and an increased premium.

Restrictions which may be attached to your policy are:

● exclusion of cover for theft or malicious damage by persons lawfully on the premises (the paying guests)

● no insurance cover for the guest's or lodger's own property

● under the liability section of your contents policy, cover for liability to domestic servants may no longer apply, if you employ them as part of your letting business.

Why insure?

When you are starting up or running a small business and every penny counts, there is a temptation to cut costs by choosing not to insure, or to deliberately under-insure. This will seem a justifiable gamble while there are no problems. But if a disaster occurs, the uninsured losses could deal your future prospects a severe blow, from which the business may never recover.

The cost of adequate insurance cover is the price to be paid for peace of mind.

What insurances are needed?

Virtually every aspect of a business can be covered by insurance. Premiums are high for some covers, but for any business insurance they are deductible expenses against tax.

You will need to consider whether the following types of insurance are necessary, or advisable, for your business:

1. **Employer's liability** – the law demands that everyone on your payroll (except family and domestic servants) must be covered by this insurance. A current certificate of insurance has to be displayed at the workplace.

2. **Material damage** – important aspects of a business you should insure include:
    ● business contents, including stock
    ● goods in transit (either by post or by transport)
    ● goods kept on other premises.

3. **Consequential loss** – loss of profits should your business cease trading due to an insured event.

4. **Public liability** – to cover your legal liability for injury to the public by you, or one of your employees' activities at work.

5. **Product liability** – to cover your liability arising from faults in products you have manufactured or serviced. For example, a machine you have repaired gives someone an electric shock.

6. **Motor vehicle and driver.**

7. **Business money** – see Figure 3 for an example of typical cover provided by a business money policy.

8. **Key person** – cover to protect the business against loss of key personnel.

Professional advice

Before reaching any final decisions on your business insurances, seek professional advice, as this complex area of insurance is full of pitfalls for the inexperienced. An insurance broker or consultant specialising in commercial insurance will discuss your requirements with you, and offer advice.

CHECKLIST

Household buildings insurance

● Check the insurance policy definition of 'buildings' covers all parts of your property.

● Note any buildings which do not conform to your policy standard construction details, and inform insurers.

● If you have a mortgage, ask to inspect a copy of the insurance policy.

● Notify insurers if you intend to carry out any business from home.

Household contents insurance

● Do your possessions fall within the policy definition of 'contents', having regard to the listed exclusions?

● Remember to include the possessions of other family members or any domestic employees, permanently resident at your home.

● Check whether you are affected by the applicable monetary limits for certain items in the policy.

● If you intend to vacate the property for more than 30 days, check how this will affect your cover.

● Ensure you do not have several policies which overlap with each other (dual insurance).

Motor insurance

● Decide which type of cover is suitable for you and your vehicle.

● If you select comprehensive cover, check which extra benefits are included.

● Be clear as to which other people (if any), you will allow to drive your car.

● When asked to drive someone else's car, check the vehicle owner's insurance, to see if it is an 'any-driver' policy.

Insurance for a business run from home

● Have you notified your household buildings and contents insurers of the business use?

DEFINITIONS

Money	means Cash Bank Notes Cheques Girocheques Bankers' Drafts Money Orders Postal Orders Bills of Exchange unused Postage Stamps National Insurance Stamps National Savings Stamps and Certificates Holidays with Pay Stamps Credit Company Sales Vouchers and V.A.T. Purchase Invoices all the Insured's own or for which he is responsible and Luncheon Vouchers the Insured's own only whilst in his custody
Non-negotiable Money	means Crossed Cheques Crossed Girocheques Crossed Bankers' Drafts Crossed Money Orders Crossed Postal Orders used National Insurance Stamps National Savings Certificates Credit Company Sales Vouchers and V.A.T. Purchase Invoices
Money in Safe	means Money (excluding Non-negotiable Money) contained in locked safe or strongroom in the Insured's premises when closed for business
Any Other Money	means Money (excluding Non-negotiable Money and Money in Safe)

a   in the Insured's premises when open for business

b   in transit

c   in a bank night safe until removed by an authorised bank official

2

Fig. 3. Typical cover provided by a business money policy.

SECTION 1: COVER

If during the Period of Insurance

a   Money is lost destroyed or damaged by any cause

b   any safe or strongroom or cash box or when used for the carriage of
Money any case bag or waistcoat belonging to the Insured is lost destroyed
or damaged as a result of theft or attempted theft of Money

while

   i   in the Insured's premises
  ii   in transit
 iii   in a bank night safe until removed by an authorised bank official
 iv   in the dwelling of the Insured or of any person to whom such Money
     is entrusted

within or between Great Britain Ireland Northern Ireland the Isle of Man
or the Channel Islands the Insurers will indemnify the Insured by at their
option repairing replacing or paying the amount of the loss destruction or
damage

**Limits of
Liability**

The Insurers' liability shall not exceed the Limit of Liability set against any
Item in the Schedule and furthermore shall not exceed in respect of

a   Non-negotiable Money   £250,000

b   Money not contained in locked safe or strongroom
in the Insured's premises when closed for business   £200

c   Money in the dwelling of the Insured or of any
person to whom such Money is entrusted   £300

d   loss or destruction of or damage to safe
strongroom cash box case bag or waistcoat   cost of repair
or replacement

3

Fig. 3. Typical cover provided by a business money policy cont/d.

29

● Study the various forms of insurance which might be relevant to your business, and select those you need to consider.

● Seek advice from an insurance specialist before finalising your insurance arrangements.

CASE STUDIES

In each chapter, the cases of three people from different backgrounds will be examined. These individuals will be taking out insurances and subsequently making claims on their policies. We will follow their progress.

At this stage, it is time to introduce our three characters.

Noah decides to run his business from home

Noah Lott is a 35-year-old family man, with a wife and two children. They live in a large, detached house on a modern residential estate.

Noah, a surveyor, has decided to start his own practice, working from home. He converts a first floor bedroom into an office and engages a part-time secretary, Anita Filer. Clients will occasionally call at his office.

Dora needs to take out new policies

Dora Bull, a 70-year-old widow, is the sole owner/occupier of a small Victorian terraced town house. There is no mortgage.

She discovers insurances on the house and contents lapsed when her husband died, and there is no insurance cover in force. She decides to take out fresh policies.

Ella is looking for motor insurance

Ella Bent, aged 30, is a career woman who spends a considerable amount of time driving around the country, either for business purposes or for pleasure.

She acquires a new two litre saloon car, mainly for private use, but on occasions it will be used for business trips. She intends to take out comprehensive insurance for her new car.

Ella was recently involved in a motor accident while driving a company car.

DISCUSSION POINTS

1. The insurance industry has moved away from issuing almost identical policies and a tariff premium rating system to the present highly competitive market. What are the advantages and disadvantages of this move from the insuring public's point of view?

2. You have just bought a 13-year-old car for several hundred pounds. It is to be used as a run-around in your local area, but not for long journeys. You live in an inner-city area with no off-street parking.

   If you were an insurer and asked to insure this car, what conditions, restrictions or penalties would you wish to impose?

3. You decide to set up a hairdresser's salon in the ground-floor front room of your home, which belongs to your parents. Your mother will occasionally help in the salon.

   Discuss the insurances you would consider taking out, and why?

2
Selecting the Scope of Policy Covers

THINKING POSITIVE

Having decided on the property or goods to be insured, the next stage is to consider the scope of insurance cover required.

At first glance, cover provided by insurance policies appears to include nearly all likely disasters, including obscure events that most people never imagine happening to them. The inclination is to presume it must cover everything you want, with any exclusions often in small print and looking unimportant. A more positive attitude is essential to ensure you read and understand the wording *in full*. **Remember, insurance policies do not provide protection against every loss.**

CHECKING COVER

Looking at household insurances

'Standard' policies for buildings and contents issued by different insurance companies contain many common features, but there are also numerous variations. You should regard every policy as an individual document in its own right.

Having emphasised this point, most of the perils or events against which we insure are common to the majority of policies. These normally include:

1. Fire

● A claim would not be met and prosecution could follow if you *deliberately* set fire to your own property.

● Smoke or scorch damage is excluded in the absence of ignition or heat, such as emission of smoke from a faulty oil heater.

2. Explosion, lightning, earthquake and thunderbolt

● Earthquakes do occur in the UK, sufficient to cause damage to buildings on rare occasions.

3. Aircraft and other aerial devices and articles dropped from them

**4. Breakage or collapse of television and radio aerials, satellite dish
aerials, aerial fittings and masts**

● Under a buildings policy, only damage resulting from the breakage or
collapse is covered, not damage to the aerial or mast itself.

● Damage to aerials, masts and fittings is covered by a contents
policy, except for external satellite dish aerials, which need separate
cover.

5. Impact by any train, vehicle or animal

● Loss or damage caused by insects, birds or domestic pets is sometimes excluded.

6. Smoke

● This peril now frequently appears as part of the standard policy.

**7. Riot, civil commotion, labour and political disturbances, vandalism
and acts of malicious persons**

● If your home is unoccupied or insufficiently furnished for full habitation for more than 30 days, cover ceases for vandalism or acts of
malicious persons.

8. Theft, or attempted theft

● If your home is unoccupied or insufficiently furnished for full
habitation for more than 30 days, cover ceases for theft or attempted
theft.

9. Storm or flood

● Under buildings policies, loss or damage to gates, hedges or fences is
not covered.

● Damage caused by frost to buildings is excluded.

10. Falling trees

● The policy does not pay the cost of felling remaining parts of tree or its removal from site.

11A. Bursting, leaking or overflowing of water tanks, pipes or apparatus

11B. Leakage of oil from any fixed heating installation, pipes or apparatus

● Loss or damage to the tank, pipe or apparatus itself, if caused by normal wear and tear, is not insured.

● If your home is unoccupied or insufficiently furnished for full habitation for more than 30 days, cover ceases for 11A and 11B.

12. Subsidence, heave or landslip

● Subsidence (downward movement due to ground shrinkage), or heave (upward movement caused by ground swelling), has to be *of the site on which your buildings stand.*

● A substantial excess applies (usually £1,000).

Looking at motor insurance

Because **motor insurance** is a legal requirement does not mean you should treat it any differently to purchasing any other service or product. Care needs to be taken when selecting your cover. If possible, when buying a new car, discuss your insurance requirements with your insurance company or broker *beforehand*. It could save you money.

Although there are variations, the basic covers included in the three types of policies available are:

1. Third party only

● Third party covers your legal liability for death of or injuries to other people, arising from accidents caused by the use of your car on public roads or elsewhere.

● It also covers your legal liability for death of or bodily injury to passengers in your car.

● It includes the legal liability of passengers in your car for accidents caused by them (for instance, careless opening of a door resulting in injury to a passing cyclist or his property).

● Third party covers your legal liability for damage to another person's property.

● And finally, it covers your legal liability for injury to other people or damage to their property caused by a trailer attached to your car.

2. Third party, fire and theft

● Fire and theft are added to the above covers, which may include lightning, explosion and attempted theft.

● Loss of or damage to spare parts or accessories by fire and theft may also be covered, provided they are kept in or on the *insured car* or in *your* private garage.

● If your car is not normally in a locked garage at night, insurers might exclude theft cover, or make it subject to special conditions or charge extra premium.

3. Comprehensive

● This encompasses all accidental damage to a policyholder's vehicle, unless specifically excluded from the policy.

● Normally excluded from cover are depreciation, wear and tear, loss of use, damage to tyres by braking, cuts or bursts, mechanical or electrical failure, loss of or damage to the vehicle due to deception, or loss in market value following repairs.

● Included is accidental injury to yourself or your wife/husband, resulting in death, or loss of sight and/or limbs (the maximum sum payable in any one period of insurance is typically £3,000 to £5,000 but excluding suicides or persons aged 75 years or over).

● Medical expenses up to a stated amount (typically £150 per person) for injuries to you or your passengers as a result of accident involving your car are covered.

- Loss or damage to rugs, clothing and personal effects in the car are covered up to a stated sum (usually about £150).

- Windscreen and car window breakage is included within cover. (If damage is limited to glass in windscreen or windows only, there will be no loss of 'no claims discount'.)

Looking at insurance for a business run from home

The law lurks behind every aspect of insurance. Not only in the complex relationship between insurer and insured, but in the meaning of the perils insured against and the legal liabilities which insurance is set up to cover. In business, the legal aspects can be particularly important, with employer's liability and road traffic insurances being compulsory under the law. It is important to distinguish between the numerous types of insurance available.

Looking at the policy covers to be considered, note the following points:

Employers' liability

Under the **Employers' Liability (Compulsory Insurance) Act 1969**, every employer carrying on a business, trade or profession in Great Britain must take out and maintain insurance against liability for bodily injury or disease sustained by his employees arising out of their employment.

- A certificate of insurance has to be displayed at the employer's premises.

- Indemnity (sum claimable under the policy) is usually unlimited.

- Although insurance is compulsory, an employer is not automatically liable for any injury to an employee. An employee has to prove his injury resulted from:

  (i) employer's negligence
  (ii) negligence of fellow employee
  (iii) breach of statutory duty (such as Health and Safety at Work Act 1974).

Material damage

It is necessary to insure business contents against loss or damage, separately from any household insurance in force. This should cover stock, machinery, office equipment, computers, furnishings, employee's personal effects and motor vehicles (over and above the compulsory insurance required under the 1988 Road Traffic Act).

The scope of the insurance cover should include:

- physical damage by the standard perils, such as fire, explosion and storm
- theft
- business money
- loss of, or damage to goods in transit (on the way to a customer, or a sub-contractor; in your own or someone else's vehicle; sent by post)
- loss of or damage to goods on a sub-contractor's premises.

Consequential loss (or business interruption)
A natural consequence of **material damage insurance**, this form of cover is for further losses which would occur if your business ceased, or was adversely affected by the happening of an insured event. For instance, after a fire, you might lose part or all of your revenue or profit, have to continue paying certain overhead costs, and incur additional expenditure to keep trading. **Consequential loss insurance** (sometimes still referred to as 'loss of profits') would cover these resultant losses for a stated period, usually not less than twelve months (known as the indemnity period).

Public liability
This insurance covers the business against any **liability to third parties** for causing death, injury or damage to their property. Excluded are risks covered by other types of insurance, such as employer's liability and road traffic insurance.

1. **Premises**: In relation to the business part of your premises, such liability might arise from:

- escape of dangerous things from your land/buildings, such as pollution

- dangerous premises – under the Occupier's Liability Act 1957, the occupier of a premises owes a duty of care to visitors, to ensure reasonably safe premises for the purpose for which visitors are invited.

2. **Employers**: At law, risks arising from the actions of employees and agents are known as 'vicarious liability'.

An employer is liable for the negligent acts or omissions of his employees, causing death, bodily injury or damage to property during the course of their employment.

Product liability
Claims made against you arising from the production or servicing of a faulty product, either under such statutes as the Consumer Protection Act 1987, or the Sale of Goods Act 1979 (amended 1995), or in negligence, could bankrupt the business. To give protection against these risks, a business can take out a **product liability** insurance policy. Cover is often expensive but increasingly necessary in this age of huge court awards.

Professional indemnity
Suppliers of a service are obliged, by virtue of the Supply of Goods and Services Act 1982 and common law, to use reasonable skill and care in carrying out their duties. Professionals are under an even higher duty, and increasingly, they find themselves facing large claims for damages in today's consumer-led society.

Protection by way of **professional indemnity insurance** is available to tradesmen and other providers of services, as well as the traditional 'professionals', like solicitors and doctors, but it is costly.

Motor insurance
Third party insurance is compulsory under the Road Traffic Acts, but it is wise to extend the cover beyond that required by the law, as employees will be driving in connection with your business.

● If your vehicle(s) is to be driven by employees, make sure you have an all-drivers policy.

● Ensure the proposed business use of your vehicle is properly and fully described in the certificate of insurance.

● Although not required under the 1969 or 1988 Road Traffic Acts, it would be prudent to insure your liability as employer, for damage to your employee's personal property arising from the use of a vehicle on a road in Great Britain.

DECIDING ON ADDITIONAL COVERS

Even the most basic insurance policies provide wide-ranging cover, but you may wish to extend your policy to give even better protection, even if this involves extra cost.

Looking at household insurances

In addition to the sections of a comprehensive policy providing cover against the standard perils, there is an option available to insure your buildings or contents on an **all risks** or **accidental damage** basis. Such cover is often referred to by insurers as 'super' or 'standard-plus' or 'maxplan'. These terms used in different policies do not always mean the same scope of cover.

This superior type of policy cover picks up incidents of accidental loss or damage in the home which would otherwise be uninsured, such as spilling paint on the carpet, or putting your foot through the ceiling.

Under 'standard' household contents policies, there is normally an all-risks extension offered. At extra cost, you can choose to insure certain possessions on this wider basis either in or away from the home. Most insurers divide this all-risks extension into several categories. Typically, these might be:

1. Unspecified personal effects

● Personal effects is not always defined, but what does not fall within this category is set out.

● The sum insured has to represent the maximum total value of such goods which you and your family may have on or with you outside the home.

● Possessions of all family permanently residing with you can be included.

● Cover usually applies anywhere in the British Isles; worldwide for holidays up to 30 or 60 days in any one year (this can be extended if required).

● A single article limit applies, perhaps £200.

2. Unspecified valuables

● This category includes such items as cameras, binoculars, furs, gold and silver articles, and jewellery.

● A single article limit of, say £500, is likely to apply.

● You are not expected to get individual items valued at the outset, but if a claim arises you may have to produce proof of value.

3. Specified valuables

● Each item insured has to be listed and valued individually.

● This policy section is generally for jewellery, curios, stamp or coin collections, pictures, expensive camera equipment and the like, with a value above the single article limit in the unspecified section.

● A valuation or receipt may be required by insurers when taking out the insurance as proof of value, and you pay the cost of valuation.

Looking at motor insurance

If you have chosen comprehensive cover for your car, it is likely that it will cater for most of the disasters which the average motorist will encounter. But there may be additional fringe benefits available, sometimes at extra cost, which you may want to consider. These include the following:

1. Up to £50,000 legal expenses cover. When you are involved in an accident where the other person is to blame, insurers will, where prospects of success are reasonable, arrange for specialists to pursue a claim on your behalf. This could be for the recovery of any policy excess, compensation for death or injuries, and for costs incurred due to loss of use of your vehicle.

2. Breakage of glass in the windscreen or windows of your car and any resultant scratching of the bodywork is an extra cover available, but increasingly, is part of the standard comprehensive policy package.

Looking at insurance for a business run from home

There are a number of covers available, which may or may not be applicable to your particular business activity. Among those covers you may wish to consider are:

1. *Director's and officer's liability insurance* – this insures the risks arising from a director or officer of the company omitting to carry out his or her duties. Examples of risks include:

● negligent performance of duties
● liability for the torts of the company
● breach of the Companies Act.

2. *Legal expenses insurance* – these vary in type, some are specialised, perhaps related to employment issues, while others are more general. Relatively inexpensive, this form of insurance is well worth considering, as taking legal proceedings can prove expensive, even when you win the case and recover most of your costs.

3. *Fidelity insurance* – this provides cover against employees stealing the company's money. A written reference will need to be taken up for each member of your staff who has access to money.

4. *Goods in transit insurance* – to cover value of goods being moved by vehicle, not normally insured by motor vehicle insurance policies.

ASSESSING THE SUM INSURED

On reading such statistics as over 654,000 homes burgled annually, we realise that disasters are happening all the time, but hope we will not be affected. If however, we do suffer a loss, there is nothing more disheartening than to find we are not going to be fully reimbursed by insurers, because our sum insured is too low.

According to a recent survey by Eagle Star Direct, the contents of nearly one home in five are underinsured. This can seriously influence the amount payable in the event of a claim. The same survey indicated that one policyholder in seven had never checked whether the full value of their possessions were covered.

The onus is always on the policyholder to fix the correct sum insured, even though we may seek advice from the insurance company or their agents.

Deciding on the current sum insured can be difficult, but if you are going to insure, make certain the amount of cover is adequate.

Insuring your home adequately

Buildings
Normally, it is a requirement of a household policy that the buildings should be insured for the full reinstatement cost (that is, the full cost of rebuilding the whole property in the same style, size and condition as when new, including outbuildings). This sum should not be confused with the market value of the property, which is probably lower.

If you have a mortgage, the mortgage lender usually stipulates a minimum sum insured, and may also give advice and guidance concerning the amount of future cover during the term of the loan. However, the final responsibility for arriving at the correct sum insured will be yours.

Annual updating of the sum insured is advised, although most are now automatically index-linked and revised when there is a variation in house building costs, as issued by the **Royal Institution of Chartered Surveyors**. If the base or starting figure is correct, under-insurance should not arise.

The Association of British Insurers publishes an information sheet

These tables prepared by the Building Cost Information Service of the Royal Institution of Chartered Surveyors, give rebuilding cost information for five different house types, related to ages, sizes and locations of houses. **Tables are unsuitable for certain types of buildings:**

Houses built of stone or materials other than brick.

Houses with more than three storeys, or basements and cellars.

Flats, because types of construction differ widely, as do responsibilities for shared parts.

Houses with special design features or of greater size than those described in the tables.

Houses containing hazardous materials eg asbestos likely to require special precaution/treatment following damage or demolition.

For any of the above categories, seek professional advice: do not rely on these tables.

Figures in the tables are based on houses of an average quality finish and might need adjusting. The figures are in respect of single glazing only. If your house is of higher quality with, for example, a luxury kitchen and sanitary fittings, floor and wall finishes, or secondary or double glazing, your final figure will need to be increased by up to 25%.

Where a fire and/or intruder alarm system is fitted, replacement costs should be taken into account when calculating your sum insured.

The regional groups are based on broad cost bands. However, local variations are caused by a number of factors including competition between builders and the ease of rebuilding.

The costs in the tables allow for re-building your home in modern materials using modern techniques. Where it is necessary for your home to be reinstated exactly in its original style - to comply with the local authority requirements, it will be necessary to allow for the additional cost and a professional rebuilding cost assessment is essential.

The tables include allowances for full central heating (at an approximate cost of £2,900), demolition costs and professional fees. The allowance for demolition costs may be inadequate if the building contains hazardous materials and in such cases a professional valuation is essential.

For garages (other than integral), rebuilding costs range between £3,000 for a single pre-fabricated to £9,000 for a double detached in brick. Using these as a guide, insert an appropriate figure against D. **Complete the calculation by estimating the cost of reinstating outbuildings, walls and fences.**

Total external area Sq ft or Sq m (upstairs and down)		=	_____	A
"Per-square foot or Sq metre" rebuilding cost		=	£ _____	B
Multiply AxB		=	£ _____	C
Add for garage (see above)		=	£ _____	D

Estimate the cost of rebuilding any outbuildings, walls and fences and any other items covered and put this figure against E

	=	£ _____ E

Now add C. D and E together = £ _____

If your policy is not index linked add on a suitable allowance for inflation   £ _____

TOTAL = £ _____

This figure is the approximate amount for which an **average quality** home should be insured.

1 London Boroughs and Channel Islands*

2 South East
Bedfordshire, Berkshire, Buckinghamshire, Essex, Hampshire. Hertfordshire, Kent, Oxfordshire, Surrey. East Sussex, West Sussex.
Scotland

3 East Anglia, North West, Northern

4 East Midlands, South West, West Midlands, Yorkshire & Humberside, Northern Ireland, and Wales.**

*Building costs in the Channel Islands are affected by local conditions and may vary from prices in this band.

**Building costs in Northern Ireland are considerably lower than in the rest of the UK and may be 20% below the costs given for Region 4.

You should seek local advice if your home is in the Channel Islands and Northern Ireland.

If you need further advice. your building society, insurance company, broker or insurance adviser will be pleased to help.

Fig. 4. House rebuilding tables.

These costings do not apply to all types of property - see overleaf.
JANUARY 1996 costings - £ / ft² gross external floor area

		PRE 1920			1920 - 1945			1946 - 1979			1980 - Date		
		LARGE	MEDIUM	SMALL	LARGE	MEDIUM	SMALL	LARGE	MEDIUM	SMALL	LARGE	MEDIUM	SMALL
DETACHED HOUSE	REGION 1	74.50	79.50	80.00	71.00	74.50	76.50	59.00	64.00	65.50	58.00	57.50	62.00
	2	65.50	70.50	70.00	62.00	65.50	67.00	52.00	56.00	57.50	51.00	50.50	54.50
	3	62.00	66.50	66.50	59.00	62.00	63.50	49.00	53.00	54.50	49.50	48.00	51.50
	4	59.50	63.50	64.00	56.50	59.50	61.00	47.00	51.00	52.50	46.50	46.00	49.50
TYPICAL AREA ft²		3450	1700	1300	2550	1350	1050	2550	1350	1050	2400	1400	950
SEMI-DETACHED HOUSE	REGION 1	72.00	73.50	74.00	76.50	74.00	74.00	55.50	58.50	62.50	60.50	61.00	65.50
	2	63.00	64.50	65.00	67.00	64.50	65.00	48.50	51.50	55.00	53.00	53.50	57.50
	3	60.00	61.50	61.50	64.00	61.50	61.50	46.50	49.00	52.00	50.50	51.00	54.50
	4	57.50	58.50	59.00	61.00	59.00	59.00	44.50	47.00	50.00	48.00	48.50	52.50
TYPICAL AREA ft²		2300	1650	1200	1350	1150	900	1650	1350	1050	1600	900	650
DETACHED BUNGALOW	REGION 1				74.50	69.50	71.50	63.50	64.00	67.00	65.00	65.50	67.50
	2				65.50	61.00	62.50	55.50	56.00	58.50	57.00	57.00	59.00
	3				62.00	58.00	59.50	52.50	53.00	55.50	54.00	54.50	56.00
	4				59.50	55.50	57.00	50.50	51.00	53.50	52.00	52.00	53.50
TYPICAL AREA ft²					1650	1400	1000	2500	1350	1000	1900	950	750
SEMI-DETACHED BUNGALOW	REGION 1				75.50	73.50	71.00	60.00	61.50	66.50	62.50	70.50	73.50
	2				66.50	64.50	62.50	52.50	54.00	58.00	55.00	61.50	64.50
	3				63.00	61.00	59.00	50.00	51.50	55.00	52.00	58.50	61.50
	4				60.50	58.50	56.50	48.00	49.00	53.00	50.00	56.00	59.00
TYPICAL AREA ft²					1350	1200	800	1350	1200	800	950	550	500
TERRACED HOUSE	REGION 1	78.50	77.00	76.50	76.50	76.50	76.00	55.00	60.00	66.50	62.00	64.00	64.00
	2	68.50	67.50	67.50	67.00	67.00	66.50	48.50	52.50	58.00	54.50	56.00	56.00
	3	65.50	64.00	64.00	63.50	63.50	63.50	46.00	50.00	55.00	52.00	53.50	53.00
	4	62.50	61.50	61.00	61.00	61.00	60.50	44.00	47.50	53.00	49.50	51.00	51.00
TYPICAL AREA ft²		1650	1350	1050	1350	1050	850	1650	1300	900	900	750	650

Fig. 4. House rebuilding tables cont/d.

These costings do not apply to all types of property - see overleaf.
JANUARY 1996 costings - £ / m² gross external floor area

		PRE 1920			1920 - 1945			1946 - 1979			1980 - Date		
		LARGE	MEDIUM	SMALL	LARGE	MEDIUM	SMALL	LARGE	MEDIUM	SMALL	LARGE	MEDIUM	SMALL
DETACHED HOUSE	REGION 1	803	858	860	763	801	822	635	687	706	624	622	666
	2	704	753	754	669	703	721	557	603	619	548	545	585
	3	669	715	717	636	668	685	530	579	588	520	518	555
	4	641	685	686	609	639	656	507	549	563	498	496	532
TYPICAL AREA m²		320	155	120	237	127	98	237	126	98	224	131	89
SEMI-DETACHED HOUSE	REGION 1	774	792	795	825	794	797	597	631	672	650	657	706
	2	679	695	698	723	697	699	524	553	589	570	576	619
	3	645	660	663	687	662	664	498	526	560	542	547	588
	4	618	632	635	658	634	636	477	503	536	519	524	564
TYPICAL AREA m²		212	153	110	125	105	84	153	125	97	147	86	62
DETACHED BUNGALOW	REGION 1				804	746	770	681	688	719	698	702	724
	2				705	654	675	597	603	631	612	616	635
	3				670	622	642	568	573	599	582	585	604
	4				641	596	615	544	549	574	557	561	578
TYPICAL AREA m²		153			153	129	94	231	123	94	177	90	68
SEMI-DETACHED BUNGALOW	REGION 1				815	790	764	646	662	713	674	758	793
	2				715	693	670	567	581	626	591	664	695
	3				679	658	637	538	552	594	562	631	661
	4				650	630	610	516	529	569	538	605	633
TYPICAL AREA m²		126			126	109	76	126	109	76	88	53	47
TERRACED HOUSE	REGION 1	843	829	825	823	823	817	594	644	713	669	688	687
	2	740	727	724	722	722	717	521	565	626	587	604	603
	3	703	691	688	686	685	681	495	536	595	558	573	573
	4	673	662	659	657	657	652	474	514	569	534	549	549
TYPICAL AREA m²		151	123	95	123	95	78	151	120	84	84	72	60

Fig. 4. House rebuilding tables cont/d.

44

which gives the average square foot rebuilding cost of various types of housing in different regions of the country (see Figure 4). The leaflets are updated from time to time and are available free from the Association at 51 Gresham Street, London EC2V 7HQ. You should also be able to obtain a copy from your insurance company, or broker.

If your house is not brick built, has unusual features, or is more than two storeys, then you may need to seek specialist valuation advice, probably from a surveyor.

The following points should be borne in mind:

● The value of the site on which the buildings stand is irrelevant.

● Some insurers adopt alternative methods of arriving at the amount of cover, such as the age of the house and the number of rooms.

● Building insurance includes permanent fixtures and fittings such as kitchen/fitted cupboards, central heating and double glazing as well as decorations, walls, gates, fences, paths, drives, swimming pools, the garage, and greenhouses.

● Allowances should be included for professional fees and demolition/site clearance costs.

Contents
When fixing the sum insured, the same principles apply as for buildings insurance. Index-linking is also available, but the consumer durables section of the retail price index is used for updating purposes.

The best way to assess the value of your possessions is to have a checklist and walk from room to room. Write down against each item the present-day cost of buying a replacement.

Most insurance companies will provide a checklist (see Figure 5), and a free Association of British Insurers information sheet is available.

Assessing values
Most policies are on a **replacement-as-new** basis (commonly referred to as new-for-old), where insurers pay the full cost of an equivalent new article when the original item is lost or totally destroyed. The sum insured should be calculated on this basis.

Less popular is **indemnity** cover. Indemnity is to place you in the same financial position after a loss as you were immediately before – neither better off nor worse off. In effect, you need to insure your goods on the basis of buying new replacements, less a deduction for wear and tear, dependent on the age and condition of the particular goods.

Claim Settlement

Your policy can be either **"replacement as new"** or **"indemnity"**.

If you have a replacement as new policy you will be paid the full cost of repairing damaged articles or the cost of replacing them with equivalent new articles if they are stolen or destroyed.

With an indemnity policy, a deduction will be made from your claim payment to account for wear, tear and depreciation.

Most home contents can usually be insured on a replacement as new basis but not clothing and household linen. What you can insure under "replacement as new" varies between insurers and sometimes age limits apply. Remember to check your policy carefully.

Sum Insured

The sum insured is the total amount of money for which your contents are covered. It is the most your insurers will pay, even if your possessions are totally destroyed - say by fire or explosion. You must insure your contents for their full value.

Some policies say that if you are under-insured, claim payments will be reduced. So remember, if your sum insured is too low you may have to pay out yourself to put things right. It is your responsibility to get the sum insured correct.

Read the following comments and use the chart to work out the full value of your home contents.

Calculating Values

Go from room to room, not forgetting the loft, garage and shed, writing down what it would cost to replace every item, new, at today's prices.

Even with a replacement as new policy, you should deduct, from clothing and household linen claims, an amount for wear, tear and depreciation. A man's suit, for example, is reckoned to have a life-span of around five years. For each year you have had your suit you should deduct one fifth of today's price of a new one. This is only a guide - the quality of property and its general condition will usually be taken into account.

Where it is difficult to establish the right figure - for example with valuables or antiques - an expert valuation may be necessary.

Enter your figures on the chart. If index-linking applies to your policy, the total is the sum insured you need. If your policy is not index-linked, add an amount for inflation during the year to come.

You may, of course, have other rooms and possessions not listed here.

	Lounge	Dining Room
Carpets, rugs and floor coverings		
Furniture: tables, chairs, stools, settees, cabinets, sideboards, bookcases. Bedroom, bathroom and kitchen furniture		
Soft furnishings, curtains and their fittings, cushions		
Televisions, videos and audio/visual equipment		
Household appliances: cooker, fridge/freezer, washing machine, vacuum cleaner, electrical goods, heaters		
Cooking utensils, cutlery, china, glass, food, drink		
Valuables: gold & silver articles, jewellery, furs, pictures, clocks, watches, cameras, ornaments, collections		
Sports equipment, books, cycles, records, computers, tapes, toys, musical instruments		
Garden furniture, lawn-mowers, ladders, tools, paint, fuel		
Household linen: table linen, towels, bedding		
Clothing		
Other items		

Fig. 5. Checklist for house contents valuation.

Kitchen	Landing Hall Stairs	Main and loft	2nd bed-room	3rd bed-room	Bath bed-room	room/ toilet	Garage & Shed	TOTALS

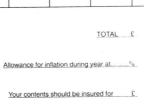

TOTAL £

Allowance for inflation during year at.........%

Your contents should be insured for   £

Fig. 5. Checklist for house contents valuation cont/d.

47

DEFINITIONS

The words listed below carry the same meaning wherever they appear in the Policy if they commence with a capital letter and their meaning is not varied by a Definition in a particular Section

Business   the occupation stated in the Master Schedule

Premises   that part of the buildings situated at the address or addresses shown in Schedule 1 and occupied by the Insured for the purposes of the Business

Business Equipment   office or surgery contents equipment Electronic Equipment fixtures fittings fixed glass and its framework external blinds and signs and all other contents (including personal effects or tools belonging to the Insured or any director partner customer or Employee of the Insured) excluding Money Business Files and landlord's fixtures and fittings

Electronic Equipment   personal computers keyboards VDUs and printers dedicated word processing equipment desk-top publishing units multi-user small business computers facsimile machines photocopiers computer aided design equipment telecommunication equipment

Business Files   account books deeds manuscripts plans drawings models maps records computer discs and tapes films transparencies or art work

Money   Cash Bank Notes Cheques Girocheques Bankers' Drafts Money Orders Postal Orders Bills of Exchange unused Postage Stamps National Insurance Stamps National Savings Stamps and Certificates Holidays with Pay Stamps Credit Company Sales Vouchers V.A.T. Purchase Invoices Customer Redemption Vouchers and unused units in franking machines all the Insured's own or for which he is legally responsible and Trading Stamps and Luncheon Vouchers the Insured's own only while in his custody

Damage   accidental loss destruction or damage

Employee   a any person under a contract of service or apprenticeship with the Insured or

                      b any person supplied to or hired or borrowed by the Insured while engaged in the course of the Business

Territorial Limits Great Britain Northern Ireland the Isle of Man or the Channel Islands

6

Fig. 6. Definitions page from a business policy (courtesy of Royal Insurance).

48

The deduction will vary from item to item, as some articles, such as clothing, depreciate rapidly in value while others, like wooden furniture, depreciate more slowly. Some pieces, for example antique furniture, can even appreciate in value.

These relevant points should be borne in mind:

1. Replacement-as-new policies normally insure clothing and linen on an indemnity basis only.

2. Some policies give 'limited new-for-old' cover, restricted to items below a certain age, typically three or five years. Other items are insured on an indemnity basis.

3. According to a survey by Eagle Star Direct, the contents of the average home are worth around £17,000. Other companies place the figure higher.

4. Sums insured should be reviewed each year at renewal date, and possibly at other times, such as birthdays, Christmas and weddings.

5. You may find it impossible to put a valuation on valuables, such as antiques, pictures and jewellery. If so, have them professionally valued, even though you will have to pay a fee.

Insuring your car

Generally, when insuring your car for the first time, the value inserted on the policy is the price paid for the vehicle. Cars depreciate quickly in value and in the event of a total loss, insurers will arrange settlement based on the market value of the vehicle, often referred to as the book value.

This value refers to the current indemnity valuation of your car, taking into account its make, age, mileage, condition and so on. It should represent your sum insured for the vehicle but in practice, the sum insured often exceeds this figure.

In certain circumstances, where a car is less than twelve months old and has received extensive damage, some insurance companies will replace the car on a **new-for-old** basis.

Insuring your business run from home

As with household insurance, business insurances are often purchased in the form of a package, which is more efficient than having separate policies for each kind of risk. Figure 6 is an example of a definition page from a business policy.

The sums insured should be revised and updated on a regular basis, otherwise you are in danger of finding a large discrepancy between the amount of your cover and the value of any loss.

Liability insurances

Sums insured for certain policies, such as employers' liability, are referred to as **limits of indemnity**. For this type of liability cover, indemnity is usually unlimited.

Other liability insurance, such as **public liability, product liability** and **professional indemnity** have substantial limits of indemnity, over £1 million not being unusual. This level of cover is needed in view of the present size of court awards.

The amount of indemnity required by your business should be assessed and discussed between you and your insurer/broker. This will depend on various factors, such as the nature of the business, turnover, location, number and type of staff.

Motor insurance

As for business use of vehicles, your insurance company or broker will guide you on the appropriate amount of cover you need under each section of your policy.

Buildings insurance

The sum insured on your buildings will be taken care of under your household buildings policy, but make sure that insurers know that part of the premises is being used for business purposes.

Should you erect any extensions or outbuildings solely for business use, these will have to be insured separately under a business policy.

Contents insurance

Under your contents policy, it is prudent to individually specify each **valuable** item of machinery or equipment including computers, and insure on a full new replacement cost basis. Other lower-value equipment needs to be carefully valued on the same basis, but with one sum insured to cover the whole.

If stock is involved, this is always valued on an indemnity basis. Fixing an adequate sum insured for this item can be difficult for some business-es, especially manufacturing concerns where there are part finished goods and goods allocated to customers, but not yet paid for. However, it is best to err on the side of caution and insure for say 10 per cent more than your calculated figure.

Loss of profits insurance

Business interruption (loss of profits) is one area where you invariably need to seek professional advice in arriving at a sum insured. Your accountant is the best person to consult.

Factors which frequently cause confusion when arranging the level of cover are:

● The sum insured is usually based on the annual gross profit, revenue or income – the policy definition of whichever term applies often differs from the way that same term is used in your business accounts.

● Last year's business accounts are used to arrive at a sum insured, but any loss which occurs will arise in the current year's trading – so the sum insured has to allow for any upward or downward trend of the business.

THINKING ABOUT THE COST

Insurance has to be **cost-effective**, so we have to constantly re-evaluate the cover and our needs, as our responsibilities, resources, commitments and lifestyles change.

While we can shop around to obtain quotations from different insurers, certain factors influence the amount of premium we are asked to pay, whichever insurer we choose. Some of these are common to all insurance companies, but others are peculiar to perhaps one or two companies. In today's changing market, the trend seems to be for insurance companies to adopt alternative ways of calculating premium rates, using various types of discounts, possibly based on lack of claims submitted, age or place of residence.

Comparing quotations received for the same risk from several insurers can be difficult, due to these differing approaches. Even where we find a very reasonable premium for the cover needed, there is every chance the premium will sharply rise the next year, necessitating a fresh review.

Aside from what the insurance companies may wish to charge, there is also the question of what we, as policyholders, can afford. Insurance has become far more expensive in recent years, and with minimum premiums payable for some policies, the cost of insurance has been beyond some people.

Most insurance companies now operate instalment schemes, usually on a direct debit system. This will probably work out more expensive than paying the whole premium in one go, so always check how much extra is payable.

Factors affecting premium rates

Common factors, other than the sum insured, which can affect premium rates are:

SECTION 2 - INTERRUPTION OF THE BUSINESS

DEFINITIONS

Revenue   the Insured's charges for work done in the course of the Business

Indemnity Period   the period beginning when the Damage occurs and ending not later than
                       the period of months specified in the Maximum Indemnity Period in
                       Schedule 2 during which the results of the Business shall be affected in
                       consequence of the Damage

A   COVER

If the Business carried on by the Insured at the Premises is interrupted
or interfered with because of Damage to any building or other property
used by the Insured at the address shown in Schedule 1 by a cause specified
in Section 1A - Contents the Insurers will pay for the loss of revenue or
additional costs reasonably incurred by the Insured during the Indemnity
Period in accordance with CLAIMS SETTLEMENT of this Section

Provided that when the Damage occurs there is insurance in force covering
the Insured's interest in the building or other property at the Premises
against such Damage under which

a   payment has been made or liability admitted

or

b   liability would have been admitted but for the exclusion in such
    insurance of losses below a specified amount

B   ADDITIONAL COVER

The cover provided by this Section extends to include interruption of the
Business as a result of

**Prevention of
Access**   Damage to property in the vicinity of the Premises by a cause covered
                       under Section 1A - Contents which hinders or prevents access to the
                       Premises

**Disease
infestation and
defective
sanitation**   the occurrence at the Premises of murder suicide food or drink poisoning
                       vermin pests defective sanitation or any human infectious or contagious
                       disease (excluding Acquired Immune Deficiency Syndrome (AIDS) or any
                       AIDS related condition) an outbreak of which the Local or Government
                       Authority has stipulated shall be notified to them

Public Utilities   accidental failure of public supplies of electricity gas or water at the
                       terminal ends of the public supply undertaking's feed to the Premises not
                       occasioned by the deliberate act of any supply authority or by the exercise
                       by any such authority of its power to withdraw or restrict supply

21

Fig. 7. Typical business interruption cover wording.

52

1. Household insurance

- non-standard building construction (for example, timber walls, thatched roof)
- age of policyholder (lower rates and cheaper policies available for over 45s, 50s or 55s)
- no claims discounts, sometimes linked to age (often 10 per cent to 35 per cent)
- postcode of your home (large inner-city areas, such as Glasgow, London and Manchester are more expensive)
- fitting approved and recommended security devices
- long periods of unoccupancy (more than 60 days per year)
- if property is a weekend or holiday home
- a poor claims record, or if another insurer has declined to provide you with cover
- if your home is in an area vulnerable to a certain peril (for example, close to a river or stream which regularly bursts its banks).

2. Motor insurance

- age of policyholder (lower rates and cheaper policies available for over 50's – higher premiums if under 25)
- no claims discounts (up to 65 per cent for claim free period of 5 years or more)
- 'restricted driving' cover (driving of car limited to you, or you and your spouse)
- payment of voluntary excesses for certain risks (you agree to pay the first £50, for example, of a claim for damage to own vehicle).

3. Business run from home

- whether you elect to have reinstatement-as-new (new-for-old) or indemnity cover
- payment of voluntary excesses for certain risks, or increased excesses above those in the standard policy form
- what type of activities and numbers/quality of staff involved in your business (for employers' liability insurance, office workers are rated lower than construction site workers)
- what risks are included, or excluded.

CHECKLIST

Household insurance

- Understand the perils or events insured against by your policy, paying particular attention to applicable exclusions.

- Decide whether you need to take out 'all risks' or 'accidental damage' cover on either the whole of the insured property, or perhaps on certain selected items.

- Are your sums insured adequate on the chosen basis of cover (either reinstatement-as-new or indemnity)?

- Review your sums insured at least once a year.

Motor insurance

- Consider the basic covers provided by the three types of policy available (comprehensive, third party fire and theft, or third party only).

- If you choose comprehensive cover, decide whether you wish to pay for any extra benefits, over and above those included in your policy.

- Regularly review the current market value of your car, so the amount of your cover can be amended each renewal.

- Think about the factors affecting the premium you pay, and whether you can do anything to reduce the cost.

Business insurance

- Know the law relating to insurance, particularly where this is compulsory (employers' liability and road traffic).

- Check and consider all the various types of insurance relating to your business, and decide on those needed.

- For material damage insurance, select whether you would be better off with reinstatement-as-new, or indemnity cover.

- Consider what risks you wish to insure against, and whether to have increased excesses, to minimise cost.

- Seek professional advice as necessary, especially for such insurances as consequential loss.

- Make certain your basic sums insured are adequate at the outset.

CASE STUDIES

Noah arranges his own business insurances

Too busy to obtain competitive quotations, Noah asks his household insurers to endorse his household policies noting the part business use, and to send him details of their commercial package policy to cover his new business venture. He also asks his motor insurers to extend his existing policy, to allow him to use his car for business purposes.

The commercial package policy seems to cover his requirements, but looks expensive. Noah cuts the cost by not taking out cover for consequential loss. He 'guesstimates' the sum insured for his office contents.

Dora accepts the lowest quotation

Dora telephones an insurance company, to discuss her need to take out cover on her house and contents. Based on her vague assessment of values, she is given quotations based on the minimum sums insured allowable under the company's policies. Dora obtains alternative quotations (including free pens) for combined buildings and contents policies from several companies advertising special terms for over 55s.

They require no detailed lists of her possessions, simply a note of the number of bedrooms and address/postcode. Guaranteed sums insured are well in excess of the value of Dora's buildings and contents. Accepting the lowest quotation, she notifies the chosen insurance company of her wish to proceed.

Ella opts for comprehensive cover

Ella Bent leads an extremely busy life, driving 20,000 plus miles each year.

Thrilled with the purchase of her new car, she visits a local insurance broker's office and asks them to arrange comprehensive cover. In her haste, she forgets to mention the likely use of the car for the occasional business trip, but does mention the recent accident she was involved in while driving a company car.

Based on a comprehensive policy, suggested by the brokers, with the use of the vehicle noted as 'social, domestic and pleasure purposes', and Ella listed as the sole driver, a quotation is verbally given to her, subject to satisfactory completion of a proposal form. The premium is higher than Ella expected, mainly because she is not entitled to any 'no claims discount', although she is offered a 30 per cent introductory bonus.

DISCUSSION POINTS

1. When taking out household insurances for buildings and contents, many people mistakenly believe comprehensive policies cover every

type of loss or damage. How could insurance companies do more to prevent this and other misunderstandings which arise over policy wordings?

2. In what circumstances would you take out a motor insurance policy with third party only cover?

3. Which types of insurance would you consider (a) essential and (b) advisable, if you were starting a small joinery business at your home?

3
Taking Out Policies

THINKING POSITIVE

Insurance is a **contract** which you, as policyholder, enter into with your selected insurance company. In return for acceptance of your premium, the insurer will provide the agreed cover, subject to the terms of the policy, *and the disclosures and declarations made by you* in the proposal. As with all legal contracts, each term used in the policy is there for a purpose. If that purpose is not clear, get reliable advice before buying the policy.

When taking out a policy, never rely on advertising material alone. Make sure you examine and understand what you are getting for your money, especially the conditions and exclusions, whether they are in large or small print. It is too late once a claim arises.

While there are many pitfalls awaiting the naive or careless, buying insurance need not be an ordeal. Just take your time, make up your own mind about what you require and then act.

BUYING YOUR INSURANCE

There are various ways of buying your insurance, although the present trend is for insurance companies to **sell direct to the public**, cutting out intermediaries, such as brokers and consultants. Some companies, notably Direct Line Insurance, were actually set up on this direct selling basis, which has proved a financial success, with no commission payable to any intermediary.

Although there are other organisations selling insurance, such as the AA, RAC and professional associations, insurance policies can be bought from the following main sources:

- direct from the insurance companies
- through an insurance broker
- through a full-time insurance agent, or consultant
- through a part-time agent
- through a bank or building society.

Buying direct from an insurance company

You can walk into an insurance company's office and buy a policy over the counter. Alternatively, you may ask for a prospectus or proposal form or simply information. More often nowadays, policies are bought in response to mail shots or advertisements.

Buying from an insurance broker

Insurance brokers are full-time intermediaries, who are paid commission by the insurance companies for the policies they sell. Usually, you do not pay the broker for arranging your insurance.

As with other intermediaries, good insurance brokers do not just sell insurance. They provide a full service to their clients, which could include determining the risks, quantifying them, and then finding the best insurance for you.

Any person or firm using the name 'insurance broker' has to be registered with the Insurance Brokers Registration Council. Registration, renewable annually, imposes strict commitments on a broker, to:

● hold policyholders' money in a separate banking account, used only for that purpose

● have at least three year's experience in the insurance industry

● hold a current professional liability policy (to cover the broker against legal action by clients for loss of their money due to his advice or actions)

● comply with the IBRC's code of conduct.

Firms of brokers vary in size, and many specialise in different types of insurance. To obtain details of insurance brokers in your area, or further information about broking, you can contact:

The British Insurance and Investment Brokers' Association
(BIIBA),
BIIBA House
14 Bevis Marks
London EC3A 7NT

One specific kind of broker is a 'Lloyd's broker', who you would need to deal with, if you wished to take out a policy with Lloyds underwriters. No direct selling system exists.

Lloyd's is not a company, has no shareholders, and does not accept corporate liability for risks insured there. It is a society of underwriters, who accept insurance risks in order to make a personal profit. As recent events have shown, they can also make substantial losses, for which they are personally liable. Restructuring of Lloyd's is now under way to protect the underwriters or members, who are grouped into syndicates, against ruinous personal losses in the future.

A Lloyd's broker does not deal exclusively at Lloyd's, but also transacts business with insurance companies.

Buying from a full-time insurance agent/consultant

Although a term like **consultant** or **advisor** may be used, really these are all **agents** selling the same products as an insurance broker, for the identical premium.

Most agents sell the policies of a number of insurance companies, for which they hold an agency. There are also **tied agents**, working directly for insurance companies, who are paid either on a commission only basis, or salary plus commission (usually restricted to one company only). The advice of tied agents is of limited value when comparing policies.

The Association of British Insurers (ABI) has a code of practice for all intermediaries, other than registered insurance brokers. It is a condition of ABI membership that companies undertake to enforce the code of their agents. The code includes strict general sales principles.

Buying through a part-time agent

These agents are often professional people, such as solicitors, estate agents, or accountants, who adopt insurance agencies as a natural sideline. They are usually agents for one or two insurances companies. Their knowledge of the market varies.

Other part-time agencies like the local garage or shop, are being phased out. Even so, you may still buy holiday insurance from a travel agent, or a furniture removal/storage insurance from a removal company when moving home, but there is unlikely to be any choice of insurer.

Buying from a bank or building society

Most major **banks** have their own insurance services divisions, registered as brokers, who provide a full range of policies, operating in the open market. In some instances, the bank may have arranged special policies or packages with insurance companies, or Lloyd's, on terms attractive to the bank. These are often sold under the bank's name or chosen description, such as 'Value Cover' (Lloyd's Bank). The underwriting insurer's name should be printed on the literature.

Anyone may use the bank's insurance services, although the schemes are chiefly aimed at the bank's customers.

For Office Use Only

Quotation Ref ....

Premium .... (inclusive of IPT)

Authorised by ....

♛ Royal Insurance

SPECIMEN
HOMESHIELD PROPOSAL FORM

A policy book with full policy wording is available on request.

Please complete in block capitals using an ink pen throughout and tick the appropriate boxes clearly. It is important that every question is completed honestly and accurately. Failure to do so may result in your claim not being paid and could lead to legal proceedings.

Full Name | Mr/Mrs/Miss/Ms

Address of home to be insured

Postcode

Address for correspondence (if different from above)

Postcode

Home Telephone No. | Insurance required for 12 months from | am/pm on | / /

Precise occupation (including any part time or casual and nature of duties) | Your Date of Birth | SPECIMEN | Your Spouse's Date of Birth - | / /

PLEASE ANSWER ALL THE FOLLOWING QUESTIONS

	YES	NO
1. Is your home		
(a) Built of brick or stone with a slate or tile roof?	☐	☐
(b) Self-contained with a separate lockable entrance under your sole control?	☐	☐
(c) Used solely as private living accommodation for you and your family (i.e. not used in any part for any business activities)?	☐	☐
(d) Furnished for full occupation?	☐	☐
2. Is your home		
(a) Left regularly unattended due to all adults being in full-time work or education?	☐	☐
(b) Left unoccupied for more than 35 consecutive days?	☐	☐
3. Has your home or any building nearby been damaged by subsidence, heave or landslip, or does it show any signs of cracking or bulging of walls?	☐	☐
4. Have you or any member of your household		
(a) Suffered loss during the last 5 years from any of the events you wish to insure?	☐	☐
(b) Been convicted of, or have any prosecution pending for any criminal offence (other than a driving offence)?	☐	☐
(c) Been refused the issue or renewal of insurance or had special terms or conditions applied or cover cancelled for any of the events you now wish to insure?	☐	☐
(d) Previously held insurance for any of the events you now wish to insure?	☐	☐

i) If 'YES', please tick box to confirm that you have attached your latest renew**SPECIMEN** .... ☐

ii) If 'YES', how many years have you been insured with this Insurer? .... [   ]
N.B. We may contact your previous Insurer to verify information.

5. Is your home   a house ☐   a bungalow ☐   a flat ☐
If a house or bungalow is it   detached ☐   semi-detached ☐   terraced ☐

6. How many bedrooms is your home designed to have? .... [   ]

7. When was your home originally built   Pre 1871 ☐   1871–1919 ☐   1920–45 ☐   1946-79 ☐   1980 onwards ☐ [   ]

8. How long have you lived in this home? ....

If less than 3 years, please state previous address

Postcode

9. Do you own your own home? (Answer 'YES' even if you have a mortgage) .... ☐ ☐

10. You will automatically be responsible for the first £50 of each claim for loss or damage to property if you choose cover for Contents or Personal Possessions (except 2. Specified Items). Do you wish to reduce your premium by paying an additional amount for each claim for loss or damage to property? .... ☐ ☐
If 'YES', please tick box to indicate the agreed additional amount. This excess will apply to all covers, except Legal Expenses.
£25 ☐   £50 ☐   £100 ☐
(for Subsidence damage to the Building a minimum £1,000 excess applies).

IF YOU HAVE TICKED ANY OF THE SHADED BOXES PLEASE GIVE FULL DETAILS IN THE 'ADDITIONAL INFORMATION' SECTION AT THE END OF THIS PROPOSAL FORM.

Fig. 8. Extract from a typical household proposal form.

Similarly, **building societies** have entered into the general insurance field. In the main, they market special insurance schemes under their own created policy name (for example, 'Homecover Plus' – Cheltenham and Gloucester building society) mostly for household buildings and contents. These schemes are underwritten by insurance companies, with the building society acting as the intermediary. In some cases, the societies have negotiated better terms for their policies, than those given by the insurance company's own policy.

COMPLETING THE PROPOSAL FORM

Insurance contracts differ from other contracts, as they are based on the doctrine of 'utmost good faith'. This places the insured under a duty to *act* with utmost good faith towards the insurer.

In particular, you must inform the insurer of all material facts relevant to your application for insurance. This means *anything* that would influence an insurer, either regarding acceptance of the risk, or the premium to be charged.

Failure to disclose a material fact enables the insurer to avoid liability for a claim, even where you thought the fact irrelevant. If it goes to the heart of the matter, a prudent insurer might have declined to offer cover, or issued cover on different terms.

The message is be very careful, and absolutely honest and frank, when filling in proposal forms.

Understanding proposal forms

A **proposal form** is intended to provide insurers with all the information needed about the risk they are being asked to insure. Such a form is required for almost every type of insurance. It provides the basis of the contract. See Figure 8 for an example, it is an extract from a household proposal form.

There is a wide variation of proposal forms between different insurers and types of insurance. Whatever style of proposal form is given to you, before completing it, request a copy of the **policy document** and read it carefully, making sure you understand even the difficult bits. If you are not clear, seek clarification from the insurer or your broker/agent.

Some questions common to all proposal forms, and others usually present include:

● full name and address

● profession or occupation (some occupations are considered to make the insurance risk more hazardous)

- occupation of spouse (this is sometimes asked for certain insurances, to avoid a person covering up a hazardous occupation by taking out insurance in the partner's name)

- your insurance history (prospective insurers may wish to contact previous insurers if further investigations required)

- has any insurer declined a proposal? (if the answer is 'yes' and you know the reasons, state them)

- have any insurers required an increased premium or imposed special conditions? (to be relevant, any such penalty must be personal to you, such as a motoring conviction)

- has any insurer cancelled or refused to renew a policy? (this would be a serious admission to have to make. It could denote a poor claims record)

- have you suffered any losses in respect of any of the risks proposed within the last . . . years? (this would include not only incidents where you submitted a claim, but also those for which you could have claimed – answers to this question may affect the premium charged, or special conditions may be imposed).

Signing the declaration

A the foot of the proposal form is the **declaration** that, to the best of your knowledge and belief, the answers to all the questions are true and you have not omitted, misrepresented or withheld any information which may be relevant.

When you sign this declaration, you are bound by it, even if someone else, such as your broker or agent, filled in the form for you. **So, check it thoroughly before signing** and **remember**, if there is a wrong answer *you* will be the loser, *not* the broker or agent.

Keep a copy of the completed proposal form, as it may be useful either at renewals, or if you make a claim.

Dealing with acceptance or declinature

Once the proposal form is completed, if your application is **accepted** you will be informed of the **premium** to be paid and any special conditions imposed on you. If given to you orally, note the **name of the person** giving it, any **reference number** and the **date**.

As soon as you say 'yes' to a firm quotation, a **contract** exists. In insurance, payment of the premium is the usual means of saying 'yes'.

It is important to realise that completing and signing a proposal form commits you to nothing. You can complete any number of proposal forms and proceed with none of them. There is no contract without your acceptance of the insurance terms offered.

Should your proposal be declined, ask the reasons, although insurers do not have to tell you. Firm refusal probably means you or your broker will have to scout around the marketplace looking for another insurer to take on your cover. A risk turned down by one insurer may be snapped up by another without any problems.

The fact is, there is usually an insurer somewhere prepared to take on a poor risk – but at a price!

DEALING DIRECT WITH INSURANCE COMPANIES

Having decided to proceed with the selected insurance, payment of the premium can be arranged in various ways.

The annual premium can be paid in cash over the insurance company counter, when a receipt should be obtained. Alternatively, payment can be made by cheque or credit card, either in person or by post. Some premiums are payable by banker's order or direct debit, a system favoured by most insurers.

To assist policyholders struggling to pay premiums in one lump sum, insurers offer **instalment plans**. Generally, these are arranged on a **direct debit** system so you must have a current bank account. A minium premium for payment by instalments is likely to be £50.

Plans vary considerably as regards cost, and the number of payments over which your premium can be spread – five, ten or twelve are common.

Before adopting this method of payment, check the final cost involved. There will be a service charge, either a percentage of the premium, a set sum per £100 or a flat fee.

Changing your mind

If you have paid your first premium, but then decide there has been a mistake and you do not want the policy, tell your insurers immediately. If you do this in reasonable time, you should get your money back, less a charge for administration costs and any time insurers were on cover.

If, after paying the premium and receiving your policy, you find the insurance is no longer required (for example, you sell the insured jewellery or car), you should inform the insurers immediately.

Should it be the first year of the policy, insurers will usually deduct a relatively high 'time on risk' charge at short-term rates, and refund the remainder of your premium. During the second or subsequent years of the policy, you may be allowed a full pro rata refund, as insurers will not have been involved in supplying the costly services of issuing a quotation and policy documents.

With a motor insurance policy, this can be **suspended** rather than **cancelled**. While you do not get your money back, it can prove a more economical option than cancellation if you intend to acquire another car.

USING AN INSURANCE BROKER

An **insurance broker** has access to a wide range of insurers. Although you pay all monies to the broker, he does not invoice you for his services. He obtains payment of his fee from the insurer by way of commission, calculated on the value of the business.

The broker is *your* agent. If he incorrectly fills in the proposal form on your behalf, you may be uninsured. However, if the mistake was his fault, you may be able to sue the broker for breach of contract.

Using a broker can be particularly beneficial when you are starting up a small business. While any major insurance company covers the normal scope of risks which most businesses insure against, you cannot be sure that the terms they offer for each category of insurance are best.

A broker's knowledge of the marketplace should enable him to get the best deal for each category.

Sometimes, if a broker arranges a policy for you, he may charge a fee, referred to as 'initial charges' or 'administration charge'. This should be shown separately from the premium.

Any advice or service from a broker, beyond the issue and continuation of the policy, is really an extra, and chargeable. Your broker may handle a claim for you, but he will probably expect to be paid for the service. Find out initially whether there will be a charge, and how much.

Should you decide to cancel a policy the broker has arranged during its first year, the broker may make a small handling charge for time spent and expenses.

USING AN AGENT/CONSULTANT

Apart from some tied agents, using an **agent** or **consultant** is much the same as using a broker. The agent may act for the insurer or the insured.

Some agents do no more than introduce their clients to the insurance companies, while others provide a similar service to registered brokers. When approaching an agent, check the extent of services offered and the terms of business, as they can vary considerably.

RECEIVING AND RENEWING YOUR POLICY

Taking precautions

Your newly purchased **policy** should be sent to you within a month or so. If not received, check with whoever you arranged the cover that it is in force.

Once received, carefully check it against your copy of the **completed proposal form**. Refer any errors to the insurer immediately.

Keep the document in a safe place and note the **policy number** in your diary for reference purposes.

Understanding the documentation

Most policies are on a standard form and not individual to you. A separate sheet, known as **the schedule**, containing your name, address, policy number and main details of the property covered with the sum insured, accompanies the policy form or booklet.

The schedule often identifies a list of items in the standard policy which you are not insuring.

For easy reference, with a pen or pencil, delete those uninsured items in the standard policy form as indicated in the schedule.

Endorsements (extra paragraphs) may be added to your policy, containing special **warranties, conditions** or **exclusions** relative to your particular circumstances. The schedule and any endorsements override the standard policy terms.

Should there be any ambiguity in the policy wording, this would be construed against the insurer by a court of law, as the insurer drew up the document.

Renewing your policy

Most policies are annual contracts, so that each year your insurance company (or broker/agent), will issue to you a **renewal notice**. Be sending out a renewal notice, insurers are offering to continue the insurance for a further year (provided there are no changes in your circumstances), subject to the terms stated.

Check any changes made by insurers, and if they are not to your liking, ask for an explanation. Also, you should advise any alterations in your situation, as you are still subject to the duty of disclosure, the same as when you completed the original proposal.

Renewal time gives both insurers and insured the opportunity to withdraw from the particular insurance. Apart from the new premium, you should consider:

- the speed of insurer's response to any claims submitted
- are there any improvements in the policy terms, and at what cost?

If you decide not to renew the policy, you need take no action. The policy will automatically lapse, but it would be courteous to inform the insurance company or your broker.

Should there be no queries or changes for you to notify, return the renewal notice with the premium payment.

Renewal notices sometimes give 15 'days of grace' for payment of the premium, following the expiry date of the policy. When days of grace are allowed, insurers would have to meet any claim arising in that period, provided the premium is paid within those 15 days. An insured not intending to renew cannot count on the additional 15 days of cover.

There are no days of grace with motor insurance.

CHECKLIST

Buying your insurance

● Decide if your best interests will be served by buying your policy from an insurance company direct, or from an intermediary.

● If you choose to buy through an intermediary, ask what other services they provide, and at what extra cost.

● Establish if the intermediary is tied to any particular insurance company or companies.

● Ask if the intermediary belongs to any organisation, such as the British Insurance and Investment Brokers' Association.

● If required, can you pay your premium by instalments, and if so, how much extra it will cost per year?

Completing the proposal form

● Disclose *all* material facts relevant to the insurance applied for.

● Once you have signed the declaration at the foot of the form you are bound by it, even if someone else filled in the form for you.

● Always keep a copy of the completed proposal.

● Completing and signing a proposal form does not commit you to that insurance policy.

Receiving and renewing your policy

● Check the policy against your copy of the proposal form, and notify any errors immediately.

● Keep your policy in a safe place.

● Cross-refer the information shown in **the schedule** against the standard policy form or booklet, to ensure it is fully understood and correct.

● When your renewal notice is received, look for any alterations to the previous terms.

● Advise any relevant change in your circumstances to insurers.

● Should you wish to renew your existing policy, send off the renewal notice with your payment.

● There is no necessity to take any action if you decide not to renew, as the policy will then lapse.

CASE STUDIES

Noah is in too much of a rush

Noah receives a proposal form to complete for the commercial package policy he is to take out.

As usual, Noah is rushed off his feet and has little time to read the form properly. Also, he is anxious not to raise any issues which might prolong the process.

The question asking for details of any previous losses within the last five years causes Noah a problem. There were several thefts of his personal surveying equipment for which he had claimed, but it would take him hours to find the dates. He decides to write 'None', as they were only minor losses anyway.

After submitting the completed proposal form to the insurance company for the second time (he omitted to sign and date the form on the first occasion), Noah receives their quotation, which he accepts. He sends off the required cheque and receives the policy a few weeks later. Noah asks his secretary to file it, without checking the document.

Dora takes advantage of available discounts

Dora receives a brief and simple proposal form which she carefully fills out and signs. Dora returns the form to the insurance company, electing to pay her premium on a monthly direct debit basis. The extra cost compared to one lump sum payment per year is 6.75 per cent.

On receipt of her policy, Dora checks the schedule against the completed proposal form. She finds no errors, but notices mention of a 15 per cent discount if the home is protected by an approved intruder alarm, or if she is a member of a police-approved neighbourhood watch scheme. As Dora is a member of a local, approved neighbourhood watch scheme, she notifies her new insurers and receives the further discount off her premium.

Ella thinks her motor insurance is sorted

Ella, having decided to accept the insurance company's quotation, walks round to her broker's office. In her company, they fill out the proposal form for her, based on the information previously given to them by Ella. Once more, the question of occasional business use for the new car is not mentioned.

Ella writes out her cheque for the first premium, which the brokers confirm will be sent off with the completed proposal form to insurers. They foresee no problems and inform Ella her policy should be sent to her in a month or so. In the meantime, they provide a 60 day temporary cover note.

Ella leaves the broker's office, her mind focused on driving her new speedster, with the insurance hassle behind her – or so she thinks!

DISCUSSION POINTS

1. What are the advantages and disadvantages of buying insurance direct from insurance companies?

2. In relation to proposal forms, do you think it fair that non-disclosure of a material fact can invalidate a policy, even where the proposal contains no specific question relating to that particular fact?

3. In what circumstances do you think it should be possible to obtain either a whole or partial refund of your premium?

4
Taking Action After a Loss

THINKING POSITIVE

The majority of us will be fortunate enough not to suffer any mishap necessitating an insurance claim in the coming twelve months. But, according to government statistics, over 1,400,000 burglaries and 63,000 fires occur annually, leaving aside all other types of losses. Even if you avoid such problems in the home, with 18.4 million men and 13.2 million women motorists on our roads today, there is an increasing likelihood of involvement in a motor accident.

This may all sound alarmist, but each year a great many people are faced with some form of loss or damage, and the resultant insurance claim. Being prepared and able to deal with such a distressing situation in an efficient way, is not only reassuring, but correct actions taken at the outset will prove beneficial in the longer term.

As with all aspects of insurance, it pays to take a positive attitude and make things happen.

CHECKING YOUR POLICY COVER

When a loss or damage occurs, examine your insurance policy to check that you are covered, before taking any hasty action. All policies clearly set out what risks you are covered against, but other aspects may not be so straightforward.

Household policies
There is often confusion when a loss occurs in the home as to whether an item is buildings or contents. This is particularly relevant when buildings and contents are insured with different companies.

As a general guide, your buildings policy covers the structure of your home with its fixtures and fittings and internal decorations.

Your contents policy covers the portable possessions you would take with you if you left home.

If you are not sure which policy to use, refer to your buildings and contents policy booklets for contact telephone numbers, and discuss the issue with both insurers.

In most cases, it should be clear whether or not you are covered for the event which has occurred, although there may be certain details requiring clarification. Try to sort out the extent of your claim entitlement, and make a separate list of areas of doubt, which you will need to raise with insurers.

Motor policies

With most motor accidents, it is not possible to check your policy until after the incident. However, every driver should know the basis of his cover (comprehensive, third party fire and theft, or third party only). Also, a driver ought to be familiar with the course of action to take at the scene of the accident. An Association of British Insurer's leaflet advises you to:

1. Obtain name(s) and address(es) of other driver(s) involved.

2. Note other vehicle registration number(s) and make of vehicle.

3. Ask for name of their insurers and policy/certificate number.

4. Note names and addresses of any independent witnesses.

5. Make a rough diagram of the accident.

6. If anybody is injured, produce your certificate of insurance (this should be produced to the police as soon as possible, and within 24 hours).

7. If there is injury to any person or animal or damage to another vehicle or other property, give your name and address, the name and address of the owner of the vehicle you are driving and its registration number, to anyone who has reasonable grounds for wanting them.

8. Note any statement made at the scene of the accident by any of the parties, but do not discuss who was at fault as this may prejudice your insurer's position.

9. Make a note of the precise location and time of the accident.

Business policies

There are likely to be a number of different insurances involved in a commercial type loss, probably placed with various insurance companies. In many instances, the insurance will have been handled by an insurance broker or consultant.

If a broker or consultant is involved, the first action is to advise him of the loss, and discuss which policies are involved. These can then be read, not only to ascertain that cover is provided, but also to check the recommended procedures.

Where you have arranged the insurances direct with insurance companies, get out all your policies and study them carefully, to determine:

● what policies provide cover for the loss (not forgetting your household insurances)
● the claim procedures to be adopted
● whether any other authorities need notification (such as the police after a theft).

The main part of the policy is usually in a standard pre-printed format, and applies to all policyholders. The policy schedule makes the policy personal to you.

The schedule for each policy should contain basic yet important information, such as:

● name of the insured
● address of the insured
● nature of the business
● the period of insurance
● premiums
● the sums insured (or limits of liability)
● the policy number
● reference to any special exclusions, conditions or aspects of cover.

NOTIFYING YOUR INSURERS

When you have suffered loss or damage, responsibility for **notifying a claim** is entirely yours. Insurers require prompt notification, and frequently set down time limits.

Among the reasons why insurers insist on speedy notification are:

● In a liability claim, where an employee has been injured at work, insurers will want to take immediate statements from witnesses.

● In a motor accident claim, witnesses' statements are important and need to be taken promptly.

● In the case of theft, insurers will want to ensure the police have been informed.

● For property damage, urgent remedial or loss reduction measures may need to be authorised.

Verbal notification of a loss to insurers is a valid way of establishing a claim, but written confirmation will be required, usually by completing a claim form (see Chapter 5).

Organising emergency action - property damage

When notifying your insurers of either a household or business loss, give some indication of the extent of the loss or damage. Also, obtain authority for immediate actions you wish to take, either to minimise the loss, or to make life bearable.

Typical of such emergency measures are:

● first aid repairs to protect undamaged property against the weather, escaping water or looting (reasonable costs incurred can be included as part of your claim)

● collecting up remains of ruined goods for later examination by insurers

● protecting any salvaged articles.

It is a condition of the policy that you minimise loss whenever possible, and insurers will usually authorise required measures, even on a temporary basis. Before contemplating permanent repairs, give insurers the opportunity to inspect the damage first.

Keep invoices or receipts for any emergency repairs, so you can recover the costs as part of your insurance claim.

In the case of household policies, many insurance companies now provide **emergency helplines** for use by their policyholders. These helplines can supply you with the names of competent tradesmen for emergency repair work, as well as detailed advice to those wishing to make a claim.

Organising emergency action – motor accidents

Whether or not you intend to make a claim after an accident, you must notify your insurers. This is a condition of your policy.

The first priority after an accident has to be the safety and care of people involved. Any injuries obviously need urgent attention.

If you happen to be away from home when an accident occurs, contact the local branch office of your brokers or insurance company in that area.

Explain the circumstances, and if possible, quote your policy number. If you cannot contact a local branch, telephone or write immediately to your own branch office, or even the head office. Always follow up any telephone conversation with a letter, detailing the date of the accident, your policy number and ask for a claim form or accident report form.

Check with your insurers about getting your car repaired. Insurers may give instructions to the repairers direct.

If you give instructions for the repairs, the cost is entirely your responsibility until your insurers agree to indemnify you for the cost. Some repairers may be unwilling to accept your instructions without your insurer's authorisation, in case they refuse to pay later.

DEALING WITH ADVISORS

When a loss occurs, leading to an insurance claim, the onus will be on you to prove the loss is due to a cause or peril covered by your policy. In most cases, completion of a claim form meets this requirement.

Also, as the insured, you have to prove the amount of your loss, in cases other than personal accident or liability. You cannot simply make a claim for loss or damage without proving the value of the item. Production of a purchase receipt, a valuation or a repair invoice may be sufficient.

The majority of claims are handled by the insurance company's own claims department, who will advise whether or not you have a valid claim. If not, ask why and check for yourself. The claim handler's decision is not necessarily final.

If the loss is covered, your claim will be given a claim number, which should be used on all relevant future correspondence or conversations.

Depending on the type of claim and the circumstances, you may have to deal with a claims specialist *appointed by insurers.*

Claims inspectors

Claims inspectors are employees of the insurance company, whose job is to **investigate** claims. They will discuss the circumstances and value or losses with you, and may offer suggestions regarding measures to prevent similar future losses occurring.

At the end of their enquiries, claims inspectors will put forward claim settlement proposals for your consideration.

Loss adjusters

If a non-motor claim is sizeable, or particularly complex, and the insurance company does not have sufficient in-house expertise, they are likely to retain **loss adjusters** (chartered loss adjusters if members of the Chartered Institute of Loss Adjusters).

Loss adjusters are independent firms who specialise in claims work. Although paid by insurers, they are impartial and process claims from start to finish.

Loss adjusters will ask questions to establish the circumstances of a loss, on similar lines to the claims inspector. They report to the insurer, on completion of their enquiries, incorporating a recommended settlement figure within the report.

Motor engineers

A different procedure is adopted by insurance companies with motor claims, where motor specialists are engaged.

After an accident, it may be that the insurance company will use their own in-house engineer to examine the vehicle or its remains, generally at the garage where it has been taken.

Some companies use outside independent firms of engineers, sometimes referred to as **motor claims assessors**.

Engineers will only be concerned with damage to the car, but they may possibly ask questions regarding the direction and point of impact, or any defects in the vehicle which might have caused, or contributed to the accident. If present at an engineer's inspection, you may ask any questions, or point out anything relevant concerning the car's condition.

Once the engineer is satisfied, he agrees the cost of repairs with the repairer, authorises the carrying out of the repairs, and reports to the insurers. The report will include an assessment of the car's pre-accident condition, and comment on whether the repairs will result in making good any previous wear and tear.

Loss assessors

So far, the advisors mentioned are either insurance company staff, or outside firms appointed by the insurance company. What if you wish to appoint someone to act on your behalf?

There is nothing to stop you appointing your own representative, be it a **solicitor, valuer, engineer** or another expert. But you will be wholly responsible for the payment of any fees involved.

Should you suffer a fairly major loss, you might consider appointing **loss assessors**, to handle the preparation of your claim, and negotiate settlement.

Although you will inevitably still have to take an active part in the preparation of your claim, as only you will know the full details of what you have lost, an assessor can provide a very useful service. The assessor will relieve you of much of the workload and worry involved in compiling and negotiating a claim. This can be particularly useful if you have to continue running a business.

The aim of a loss assessor should be to ensure you receive the maximum to which you are entitled under the terms of your policy.

UNDERSTANDING THE ROLE OF BROKER/CONSULTANT

The **broker's** or **consultant's** main role is placing insurance business with insurance companies. As client, you can obtain independent advice from your broker/consultant on a wide range of matters, without direct cost to yourself. For example, you can have guidance on insurance needs, the best sort of cover and its restrictions, the most appropriate market, clarification of any policy conditions imposed by insurers, and be kept up-to-date with any relevant market changes.

When a claim arises, you should inform your broker or consultant immediately, and he will promptly contact your insurance company to advise them. You can also expect to be given advice regarding claim procedure.

Acting for you on claims

While your broker/consultant may not wish to handle your claim for you, even for an extra fee, he will probably have some commercial influence with your insurance company. This can help during **claim negotiations**.

Keep your broker or consultant fully informed regarding progress of your claim, whether it is being made on your policy or someone else's.

CHECKLIST

● Examine your policy when a loss or damage occurs, to check you are covered.

Household policies – taking action

● If in doubt concerning the extent of your cover after a loss, seek clarification from *all* the insurance companies involved.

Motor policies – taking action

● Learn the course of action to adopt at the scene of an accident.

Business policies – taking action

● If your insurances are placed through a broker or consultant, advise him immediately of any loss, and seek his guidance on procedure.

- If your insurances are arranged direct with insurance companies, examine all your policies, especially the schedules, and follow the recommended claim procedures.

Notifying your insurers

- Remember you are entirely responsible for notifying your insurers of any loss.

- Note and observe any time limits applicable for notification of claims.

- Verbal notification is sufficient, but written confirmation will be needed (usually a completed claim form).

- For property damage, seek authority to carry out any emergency work required, keeping any invoices or receipts.

- Use your insurance company's 'helpline' service, where appropriate.

- If you are involved in a motor accident, immediately advise your insurers, even if you do not intend to claim on your policy.

- Do not have any repairs carried out without your insurance company's prior approval.

Deciding on advisors

- Insurance companies may appoint specialists to deal with claims, either their own staff or outside experts.

- As an insured, you can appoint your own claim advisor, but at your own expense.

- If you have a broker or consultant, he may agree to handle your claim for you, but you could have to pay a fee.

- For a fairly major loss, you may decide to pay for the services of a loss assessor, to handle your claim from beginning to end.

CASE STUDIES

Noah acts in haste

A month after Noah's new surveying practice commences trading, his home is damaged by a storm. Rainwater penetrates the roof, cascading down through Noah's first floor office and several ground floor rooms. Damaged by the water are decorations, office equipment, furniture and furnishings and a portable typewriter belonging to his part-time secretary, Anita Filer.

Noah asks his wife to notify their household insurers of the damage, while he will inform his business insurers. At that moment, an urgent telephone call demands his attention, and it is three days before he gets round to contacting his business insurers. They promise to send him a claim form for completion, and mention their claims inspector will be calling on him shortly.

Noah, impatient as ever, goes ahead and orders replacements for the telephone, fax machine and photocopier.

Noah then discovers drawings have been ruined. He contacts a local draughtsman and arranges for him to redraw the plans, at twice the normal rates for extra speedy service, as they are urgently required by clients.

Dora immediately seeks her insurers' advice

Dora is called to the front door while cooking chips. When she returns to the kitchen, the chip pan is ablaze.

Dora turns off the electricity and smothers the pan with a fire blanket kept in the kitchen. Once the fire is extinguished, Dora throws the hot pan of oil into the garden, and then telephones the fire brigade as a precautionary measure. They check everything is safe.

Unfortunately, the kitchen area is severely heat and smoke damaged, and smoke has also spread into the adjoining hallway.

Dora telephones her household insurers, and describes the nature and extent of damage. The claims handler says a claim form will be sent in the post. In the meantime, Dora is given permission to start clearing up the mess, as long as she keeps any damaged items available for inspection.

Due to the amount of cleaning work required, the insurance company arrange for specialist cleaners to call later that day, to carry out whatever cleaning work is needed. Their initial bill will be forwarded directly to the insurance company for payment.

Ella is involved in a collision

Ella loves her new, zippy car and within the week, she uses it for a business call in North Wales.

While speeding round the narrow countryside lanes in Wales, Ella is confronted by an oncoming car. On the wrong side of the road, she tries to avoid the other vehicle, but there is a glancing collision. Both drivers get out their cars, shaken but unhurt. The two cars have sustained severe scratches and dents, and head lamps are smashed. There are no witnesses.

Ella apologises and admits the accident was entirely her fault. She says her insurance company will pay all the costs involved. Both drivers decide not to call the police, as there are no injuries.

After exchanging details, both drivers are able to drive away from the scene.

Ella takes her car to a local garage. They can start repairs immediately at a cost of about £500. She gives the garage instructions to proceed, confirming she will pay the cost. Ella hires a car and arranges to collect her own vehicle in a few days, when her business in the area has been completed.

On returning home, Ella reports the accident to her insurance brokers. She shows them the receipted repair account, as well as the car hire invoice, and intimates a claim under her policy.

DISCUSSION POINTS

1. Even though most insurance policies are now in 'plain English' style, why do you think people still find them so difficult to understand?

2. If after a loss, you discovered that, in error, you had taken out two identical policies with different insurance companies, and both provided cover for the loss, how would you proceed?

3. Discuss the advantages and disadvantages of using the services of an intermediary when faced with pursuing an insurance claim.

5
Compiling Your Claim

THINKING POSITIVE

When a loss occurs in the home, particularly one of a serious nature, the unfortunate householder or business owner is usually in a state of shock for several days. Notifying various authorities and contractors, organising clearing up operations or repairs, and generally sorting out matters can take all your time and effort. Many people feel unable to cope with even the thought of compiling a detailed claim list.

Difficult though the thought may be, it is important to take positive steps to start putting together a **list of damaged, destroyed or missing property as soon as possible,** for a number of reasons.

1. Most people have great difficulty remembering details of their possessions, though they may have been in a room for many years. The longer you leave the listing, the more likely you are to forget things.

2. After a fire, for example, burnt out remains may be disposed of quickly. If you do not make a list from the recognisable remains of objects, the chances are you will not remember some of the items once the remains have gone.

3. Counting and listing lost or ruined articles can be onerous and distressing. Delay makes the task even more difficult, and increases the temptation to leave if for yet another day. In the end, the whole claim process is held up.

The position of a motorist after a road accident or a theft is somewhat simpler. While there are various procedures to be followed, involving insurers, repairers and the police, there is no need to compile a claim schedule as such, except when a list of personal possessions or accessories is lost from the vehicle. Here, the same attitude towards the listing is needed, if your claim is to be quickly sorted out.

ASSESSING YOUR CLAIM

Organising the claim

If you are preparing and presenting your own claim, make sure you are organised and work in an orderly fashion. So many claimants, often aggrieved that they have to do the running around and prepare the claim, put forward an untidy list in a piecemeal fashion. This is counter-productive, for the following reasons:

● Scruffy, untidy lists of damage are more likely to result in errors.

● A claims handler, or some other insurance company representative, is going to struggle checking your claim, if the writing is illegible or figures cannot be understood, leading to delay.

● Duplications could easily occur in the claim, which might give rise to suspicion of fraud.

The orderly and well-presented claim comprises:

1. Neat lists of the *lost or ruined items*, either on the claim form, or on separate sheets attached to the form. Separate lists should be prepared for different policies, broken down either on a room-to-room basis, or between different groups of items, such as clothing, furniture, ornaments, toys and so on.

2. Lists of *damaged* items which are capable of being cleaned, restored or repaired, again broken down in the same way as under 1.

3. Prices or values should be placed alongside each item on the claim, making clear the basis of valuation. For example, new replacement cost, catalogue price or second-hand value.

4. Where appropriate, supporting documentation, such as builders' estimates, jewellers' valuations or suppliers' invoices should be securely attached to the claim lists.

Keep copies for your own reference of all these claim details.

Listing the losses or damage is a difficult job, but most people experience the greatest problems when **pricing the claim**.

The basis of pricing the claim depends on the type of cover you have, that is **new-for-old** or **indemnity**. In either case, you need to know the **new replacement prices**. Some suggested cost sources are listed under the following headings of household, motor and business policies.

Household policies

Buildings
- builders' or repairers' estimates/quotations
- accounts for emergency works, including those from gas and electricity companies
- fee invoices from professional experts such as surveyors and architects
- your own charges, shown as hours worked at a previously agreed rate per hour, for any work you carried out – for example, cleaning and decorating.

Contents
- valuations from experts, such as jewellers or antique experts
- estimates from furniture or furnishing suppliers or restorers
- prices obtained from shops or original places of purchase
- home shopping catalogues, which give prices for a wide range of goods.

Motor policies
- estimates from repairers (some insurers may have their own approved repair schemes, where certain selected garages can start repairs immediately)
- *Glass's guide* (annual pricing guide book used by dealers and insurance companies)
- motoring magazines (prices of new and used cars).

Business policies
- estimates/quotations from suppliers or repairers of commercial equipment and other business goods
- invoices from repairers or suppliers for emergency works to equipment
- details of accounts and trading figures from your accountants, if loss of profits claim involved.

A general tip when assessing your claim is, if in doubt, include the item in question in the claim list. There are always likely to be some doubts, such as, are my pot plants covered, or can I claim for the coat Auntie Nellie left here on her last visit? Let the insurance company delete the item if necessary, with an explanation.

OBTAINING REPAIR/REPLACEMENT COSTS

The doctrine of **good faith** should be in every policyholder's mind when setting out to obtain estimates for the repair or replacement of damaged property. Regrettably, many see an opportunity to put a little extra money in their pockets, as well as having the remedial works carried out. A favourite ploy was to have a claim paid on the basis of a reputable builder's estimate, and then have someone else carry out a cheaper repair, often with disastrous results. There is no room for profit in an insurance claim, and strictly speaking, money not spent on repairs should be returned to insurers.

To combat such problems, most property claims are now dealt with on a **reinstatement** basis, where payment is not made by insurers until the works are completed and they receive an invoice or receipt.

As for motor claims, the premiums we pay are largely governed by the cost of accident damage repairs. For some years, insurers have been concerned at the level of charges by garages, and this has led to a much tougher attitude towards repair bills.

Usually, an estimate from a motor repairer shows the costs for labour, with required new parts listed but not costed. The wording is 'parts at manufacturer's retail prices', or something similar.

Getting alternative estimates

For the majority of claims, you will have to obtain two or three alternative written estimates from different repairers or suppliers. Points to bear in mind are:

1. Make sure all estimates are priced on the same schedule of work, to make direct comparison easier.

2. If you choose to have extra work carried out at your own expense, ensure this is shown and priced separately.

3. Select repairers/suppliers who you are sure can complete the job efficiently and speedily.

4. Select repairers who have a reputation for doing a good job at a reasonable price.

5. Use the right type of contractor for the work, and do not ask a specialist carpenter to quote for a replastering and decorating job.

6. Always ask the repairers to detail precisely the work on which their price is based, to avoid the possibility of unexpected 'extras' being added to the final bill.

Using helplines

Most insurance companies now provide **helpline services** for house-holders and motorists involved in claim situations.

In the case of property damage, a free 24 hour telephone service, manned seven days a week, is usually available.

The helplines can provide you with names of competent tradesmen in your area, and other advice regarding emergency action and obtaining estimates or quotations.

As for motor accidents, the free 24 hour telephone service will often direct you to those motor repairers recommended by your particular insurance company. Figure 9 is an extract from a helpline form.

DEALING WITH PROFESSIONAL ADVISORS

Working with loss adjusters

When **loss adjusters** are retained as experts by insurers, usually at an early stage, they will process a claim from start to finish.

Although appointed and paid by insurers, loss adjusters have a duty to act impartially, adjusting claims up, as well as down. Also, they perform a useful role in giving guidance on procedure, and organising the rebuilding or repairs.

Contrary to popular belief, loss adjusters' fees are related to the final settlement figure, *not* the amount by which a claim may be reduced.

The loss adjuster will gather all the facts of the claim before reporting to insurers, with recommendations for settlement, if the circumstances are in order. The reports are solely for insurers' eyes and not made available to an insured. The final decision rests with the insurers, but they usually follow the loss adjuster's recommendations.

Before the loss adjuster calls, sort out in your own mind what you need to tell or ask him. Also, be clear as to the content of your claim, if this has already been compiled.

The sort of questions usually raised with a loss adjuster during the early stages of a claim are:

● Is there any reason why the claim should not be met in the usual way?

● When can a contractor be instructed to start the remedial works?

● How will payments to the appointed contractors be arranged?

● Is it possible to claim for own labour if a policyholder carries out clearance/cleaning, or any other work? If so, how much?

● How long is it likely to take before the claim is settled?

24 Hour Claims Assistance

Staff are available round the clock to advise you on claims procedures and answer your emergency enquiries.

Your Helpline membership card contains a special freephone number which you can ring as often as you like whenever you like.

Helpline 0800 555 333

24 Hour Legal Advice

A team of qualified legal staff is available night and day to advise you or any member of your immediate family, living with you, on any personal legal problem. You will be advised of your legal rights and what courses of action are open to you. All the advice is confidential and there are no consultation fees – all you pay for is the phone call.

Legal Advice 0738 30005

24 Hour Emergency Call-out Service

If you need a plumber, joiner, glazier, builder, roofer or any other tradesman then we can help. Our emergency home helpline is available giving access to a large number of trades and services.

No need to:

● Search through a phone book to find a tradesman

● Waste time on phone calls

● Take a chance with an untried tradesman

Just call the free helpline number and let us find a reputable, local tradesman to solve your problem.

You must pay the workman but if the damage is covered under your policy the cost will be refunded, subject to the terms and conditions of the policy.

It does not matter what your problem is, give us a call and let us take the heat out of the situation. We will also help to minimise the problem until the tradesman arrives, so don't worry about how often you need to phone, the call is free and we will be happy to help.

Free Emergency Call-out Service 0800 555 333

How to use your Helpline Card

As a General Accident policyholder you are entitled to receive the attached Helpline Card which you can use as often as you like! Simply by telephoning the appropriate Helpline number and quoting your policy number and your name, you can have immediate access at any time, to Helpline's range of round the clock services.

Please insert your policy number on the card immediately as you will be asked to quote it when you call.

Your GA Helpline Card

Policy Number

If you lose your Helpline Card

If you lose your Helpline Card, contact General Accident Helpline

Fig. 9. Extract from a helpline form.

He may not be able to give final answers to all these questions, but he should be able to give helpful replies.

Working with loss assessors

Loss assessors specialise in **preparing and negotiating claim settlements** on behalf of policyholders. They are paid by the policyholder, who is responsible for preparing and submitting a claim, and must bear any associated costs, which would include loss assessors' fees. These would not be covered as surveyors' or architects' fees, even though loss assessors sometimes provide such a service.

Normally, loss assessors are engaged for the more substantial household and commercial claims, and their services comprise:

- full and proper preparation of a claim, including a detailed check of your policy, to make certain relevant sections are drawn to the attention of insurers

- speedy preparation and submission of a claim to insurers, or the appointed loss adjusters

- settlement of the claim as quickly as possible.

If approached by a loss assessor, **check his credentials**, and find out if he is a member of the Institute of Public Loss Assessors (IPLA). You will have to pay the loss assessor a percentage of the claim he obtains for you. Sometimes, this is on a sliding scale, for example, 10 per cent of the first £1,000, but it can be a flat overall percentage, perhaps in the region of 5 per cent. In any case, you should ask for a written quotation for fees.

Appointing specialists

During the course of a claim, you may find it necessary to appoint a **specialist**, such as a **surveyor, architect, solicitor** or **valuer**. This could be to assist with reinstatement of damaged property, or to advise on a valuation or legal problem.

Some specialists' fees, for example those of a surveyor, architect or other consultant, will be covered by your buildings policy, provided they are 'necessarily incurred in the reinstatement or repair of the building'.

Whatever the circumstances of the appointment, the specialist will be appointed by you, as the employer, and you will be liable for payment of the fees, even if the insurance company is ultimately providing the funds. You, and not the insurance company, will also have to sign any repair contract involved, as the employer.

Contents

SUN ALLIANCE
INSURANCE UK

How we can help you:
Sometimes claims are delayed by incomplete information.
Please help us to help you by:
● giving clear and precise information to avoid delay
● remembering to sign and date this form
● co-operating with any future investigations.
Claims under your Sun Alliance and London Insurance plc policy
will be handled by Sun Alliance Insurance UK Ltd.

IMPORTANT
Insurers and their agents share information with each other
to prevent fraudulent claims and for underwriting purposes
via the Claims and Underwriting Exchange register, operated
by Insurance Database Services Ltd. A list of participants is
available on request. The information you supply on this form,
together with the information you have supplied on your
application form and other information relating to the claim,
will be provided to participants.

CLAIM NO.

POLICY NO.   INCIDENT DATE

1. Policy details
Name(s) of policyholder(s) (Mr, Mrs, Miss)   Address of policyholder(s)

Date(s) of birth

NOTE - Our representative may call on you to discuss this
claim. Please ensure that a telephone number is provided in
case an appointment is required. Regrettably our
representative can only make calls during the normal working
week, i.e. Monday to Friday.

Postcode

Tel no. (9am-5pm)   (after 5pm)

2. Circumstances
Please supply full details of the incident/circumstances/damage sustained. If you are able to supply a photograph of the damaged
area(s) this would be appreciated and may assist in the handling of the claim.

Person who caused the damage   Details of witnesses to incident

Name and address   Name and address

Postcode   Postcode

Is the item considered to be beyond   Has the item been examined by a
economical repair?   Yes ☐ No ☐   repairer/carpet specialist/supplier?   Yes ☐ No ☐

Don't know ☐   If **Yes**, please attach written confirmation from a qualified
specialist.

3. For carpets only

a. Description   d. Nature of damage

Plain ☐   Patterned ☐   Wool ☐   Surface pile ☐   Pile and backing ☐   Underlay ☐

Wool/Nylon ☐   Nylon ☐   Hessian backed ☐   Stain only ☐   Other - please specify ☐

Rubber backed ☐   Linoleum ☐   Carpet tiles ☐

b. Colour ☐   Light ☐   Dark ☐   e. Fixing

c. Location   On solid floor ☐   On wooden floor ☐

Lounge ☐   Bedroom ☐   Stairs ☐   Loose laid ☐   Fixed by adhesive ☐

Hall ☐   Kitchen ☐   Bathroom ☐   Fixed by nails or grippers ☐

Other - please specify ☐

Fig. 10. Typical household claim form.

4. Repair/replacement cost

Details of property damaged. Please provide as much information as possible, e.g. make/model/specification, age, condition etc.	Ownership - state details of owners identity, e.g. hired/loaned goods, items owned by tenant, Hire Purchase Co, business etc.	State where and when originally purchased, together with original price paid. Attach original documentation if available.	Estimated repair or replacement cost. Attach repair estimates.

NOTE - Please note that the policy does not extend to cover undamaged parts of sets or suites. The damaged item(s) should not be disposed of pending our investigation of the claim as they may be examined by our own representative.
If the item(s) are damaged beyond repair we may arrange for them to be replaced. If an identical model is not available our liability will be limited to the nearest equivalent model and specification.

5. Police details

Have the police been notified?   Yes ☐   No ☐   Police officer handling case

NOTE - Police must be advised in cases of theft, attempted theft, malicious damage or vandalism.

Address of police station involved

Police Reference No.

Date Notified   Postcode

6. All claims

a. Is your home or any part of your home:

	Yes	No
i. used for any business or professional purposes?	☐	☐
ii. occupied by persons other than you, your spouse, children or relatives?	☐	☐
iii. currently unoccupied or left unoccupied for more than two months in a year?	☐	☐
iv. unfurnished?	☐	☐

b. Have you or any other persons normally residing with you:

	Yes	No
i. ever been convicted of any offence other than driving offences?	☐	☐
ii. sustained any loss, damage or liability during the last five years?	☐	☐
iii. had any insurer decline or cancel or declare void any insurance or impose special terms?	☐	☐

If you have answered **Yes** to any of the questions in this section please provide further details

Please give details of any other insurance policy covering the same loss/damage

Occupation of Policyholder   Spouse

8. Declaration
I/We understand that you may seek information from other insurers to check the answers I/we have provided.

I/We declare that the above statements and information given are true to the best of my/our knowledge and belief.

Signature(s) of policyholder(s)   Date

427334 (1-95)   Sun Alliance Insurance UK Ltd No. 150650. The Registered Office is: 1 Bartholomew Lane, London EC2N 2AB

Fig. 10. Typical household claim form cont/d.

87

Royal Insurance

<table>
<tr><td>Branch Address</td><td>If you are completing this form for information purposes only rather than submitting a formal claim under your policy please tick box ☐</td></tr>
</table>

Motor Vehicle Accident Claim Form

When you complete the claim form, please write clearly in block capitals and use ink. Please sign and date the form.

Details of Policyholder | Claim No.

Name .... (Mr/Mrs/Miss/Ms)   Occupation/Business ....

Address ....   Telephone No.   Home ....

....   Business ....

.... Post Code ....   Policy or Certificate No. ....

Vehicle/Use

Make .... Model .... Registration No. ....

Year first registered .... Engine Capacity .... Chassis No. ....

Give details of any trailer and/or loose container ....

Is the vehicle, trailer or container owned by policyholder? .... YES/NO

If not give details of owner ....

Was the vehicle being used on policyholders order or with permission? .... YES/NO

For what purpose was the vehicle being used? ....

If commercial vehicle, Gross Vehicle Weight ....

Particulars of Driver

Name ....   Age ....

Address ....   Date passed driving test ....

....   Type of licence held - Full/Provisional/Heavy Goods (please delete as appropriate)

.... Post Code ....   Permitted Groups ....

If licence issued outside Great Britain, Northern Ireland or Channel Islands, state how long held .... years

If driver is not policyholder give details of relationship e.g. employee, family relation, friend ....

Has driver   (a) been convicted of any driving or motoring offence within the last 5 years or is any prosecution pending? .... YES/NO

If 'YES', please give full details including the date, offence code and penalty points ....

....

....

(b) been involved in an accident during the last 5 years? .... YES/NO

If 'YES', please give details ....

....

....

If private car, who is the main user? ....

Details of Damage to the Policyholder's Vehicle

Damage

Point of Impact: Mark XXXXXX

F [car diagram] R

(If we cover the damage to your car our Recommended Repairer Scheme offers the advantage of guaranteed repairs. Please ask any Royal Office or your Insurance adviser about the most suitable repairer for your particular vehicle.)

Is your vehicle still in use? .... YES/NO   Have you authorised repairs? .... YES/NO

Where may our engineer inspect the vehicle? ....

Are you registered for V.A.T.? .... YES/NO   What percentage can you recover? .... %

If you are registered for V.A.T. do you authorise us to instruct repairs on your behalf? .... YES/NO

(The V.A.T. content of the repair account is payable by you to the extent that you can recover the tax.)

Fig. 11. Extract from motor claim form – accident details and declaration.

Sketch. Please make a rough sketch showing road widths, traffic lights, warnings, etc., where appropriate. Indicate direction of vehicle with an arrow

Give name and address of any independent witnesses.

1. ....
....
....
Tel No. ....

2. ....
....
Tel No. ....

Circumstances of Accident

Date .... Time .... am/pm   Place: Street or Road ....

Town .... County .... Speed ....

Weather Conditions ....

Does the driver think they were at fault for the accident? .... YES/NO/Partially

If 'YES', do we have your permission to deal with the third party claim? .... YES/NO

Did the Police attend? .... YES/NO

If 'YES', give the officers name number and station

Name .... No .... Police Station ....

Have the police issued a notice of intended prosecution or given a verbal warning or caution? .... YES/NO

If 'YES', to whom and for what alleged offence? ....

Give details of what happen.

....
....
....
....
....
....
....
....
....

Particulars of Other Parties Involved and Property Damaged

Name and Address of owners and, if appropriate, driver	Make/Model Reg. No	Insurers Name, Address and Policy No	Apparent Damage
.... Post Code			

Details of Persons Injured

Name and Addresses	Nature of Injury
1. Own passengers:	
2. Others:	

Were the passengers wearing seat belts? .... YES/NO   Were the passengers employed by you? .... YES/NO

Date [   ]   Policyholders Signature [   ]   Drivers Signature [   ]

Fig. 11. Extract from motor claim form – accident details and declaration cont/d.

89

COMPLETING THE CLAIM FORM

In most cases, the claim form or motor accident report form is normally the means by which a policyholder notifies a claim to insurers. Figure 10 is a typical household claim form. The style of forms varies between different insurers, but generally, the basic information required is similar.

People tend to be frightened by claim forms, in the same way they are scared by tax forms. The secret is to keep your answers brief and to the point. Do not add unnecessary waffle, which may only serve to give your insurers reason to seek clarification, and so delay matters. As with tax forms, you will find many of the questions are not relevant to your particular claim.

If you do not understand any questions, do not make guesses. Ask your insurers, or broker for an explanation and guidance. It will save time and trouble in the long run.

A common fault in the preparation of claim forms is a failure to complete the easiest part – the signature and date at the end.

Unravelling the claim form

Household, motor and commercial claim forms contain questions, which can broadly be split into two categories.

1. The first category are questions which deal with general issues, such as name of the insured, policy number, contact address, date and situation of the occurrence. On commercial forms, there will be questions on the description of the business.

    These are important questions as regards checking whether the policy cover was operative when the occurrence took place.

2. The second group of questions have more direct relevance to the actual claim.

● *The household claim form* asks a number of questions about the nature of the loss or damage, and affords space for listing the lost or damaged items. Supplementary lists can be attached.

● *The motor claim form* (or motor accident report form) asks for full details of the accident, the drivers, the damage and any other parties involved (see Figure 11).

● *The commercial claim form* follows much the same pattern, except that the specific questions are far more detailed than the other two types of insurance. In the case of a business premises claim form, the questions are particularly extensive.

Pointing the way

The following are ten general tips regarding claim forms:

1. Do not cross out questions – if you do not know the answer, say so, explaining why you cannot answer.

2. If the form asks you to send builders' or other estimates with the claim form, and these are not yet to hand, write 'to follow' on the form.

3. There will be a question asking if there is any other policy in force which would also cover the loss. If there is duplication of cover, give the name and address of the other insurer and the policy number. The two insurers will sort out who pays what proportion of the claim.

4. On the reverse of the claim form are columns under headings, such as 'articles damaged or destroyed', 'date of purchase', 'current price', 'estimated value at time of loss', 'value of salvage', and 'net amount claimed'.

    If yours is a **new-for-old** policy, ignore all the middle columns. Simply fill in the description of the article and the current new replacement cost under the 'net amount claimed' column.

    Should you have an **indemnity** policy, you need to deduct a suitable amount for depreciation/wear and tear on each item, according to the life of the article. It will be necessary to fill out details under all the columns, but some purchase dates may, unavoidably, be approximate.

    If you are unsure about how much to deduct for age/wear and tear, do not make wild guesses, as you may under-value your claim. Discuss it with your insurer, broker, or the loss adjuster.

5. Should any item have a salvage value, insert what you are prepared to offer for the remains of the damaged article, if you are interested in keeping it.

6. If you have a motor accident but do not intend to claim, a claim form or accident report form must still be submitted to your insurers. Simply write across it, preferably in red, 'report only'.

7. On a motor claim form, in particular, your answers may well be

checked against the information you gave on the original proposal form and later renewals. Any discrepancies could create problems with the claim.

8. If you are buying the car involved in an accident on hire purchase, give insurers the name and address of the finance company. Should the car be a total write-off, this will affect who gets the insurance monies.

9. If any questions on a motor claim form seem irrelevant, write 'not applicable'.

10. When you cannot answer any questions asked about the motor accident, say you do not have the information, or you do not remember. Never guess.

PLANNING AND ACTING

With any type of insurance claim, it pays to be looking ahead, as well as keeping pace with current developments.

One of the biggest frustrations is delay, and so often this happens because of a lack of forward planning and organisation by the insured.

At the time of preparing your claim, there are a number of matters you can be attending to. These are listed under the following headings of household, motor and business insurance.

Household insurance

1. If rebuilding works are involved, consider whether it might be a good opportunity to carry out those alterations or additions to the layout you had discussed in the past. Insurers will still pay the cost of reinstating the damage in the original form, even if you decide to use the monies to reinstate in a different form. The cost saving on your 'own works' could be substantial.

2. Should there be any cleaning required, perhaps due to smoke soiling of clothing and linen, go ahead and take these articles to professional cleaners. Insurers will pay for such work as part of your claim, provided you obtain a receipt. They support any attempts to minimise a loss.

3. If your home is rendered uninhabitable following a loss, the reasonable cost of alternative accommodation for you and your family is

covered by both household buildings and contents policies. You will have to find suitable accommodation, to a standard comparable to that of your home. But insurers will not pay for such costs as food, which you would have had to buy anyway. The amount of any savings realised while you are living away from home, such as gas and electricity, will be offset against the accommodation cost.

Many insurers will also pay for your dog to be temporarily housed in kennels.

There are financial limits under each policy for alternative accommodation, based on a percentage of the sum insured, usually between 10 and 20 per cent.

4. Where contractors' or suppliers' estimates/quotations are still awaited, keep chasing them. Tradesmen and other business people may be first class at their jobs, but are frequently inefficient with their paperwork.

5. If your home is mortgaged to a building society, inform them immediately of a loss. You would have to do so anyway, if the society arranged your insurance. Should they wish to get engaged in the claim negotiations, it will give them time to set up their arrangements.

Motor insurance

1. Check with your insurers whether they will be giving instructions direct to a repairer. Plan to keep chasing them, if necessary, on a regular basis.

2. Where a repair is involved, find out from insurers, or their motor engineer, if any costs will be your responsibility, and why. Arrange to have your own expert check the vehicle, if you intend to dispute the engineer's findings.

Business insurance

1. On any hired, leased or business equipment subject to hire purchase, immediately contact the owners or finance company, to advise them of the loss/damage. Confirm your understanding of the insurance arrangements for the equipment with them, after you have checked your copy of the contract.

    If appropriate, ask the owners for written confirmation of the written-down value of the equipment involved, for inclusion in your claim.

2. Following a loss:

● notify all your customers/clients if it involves them or their property, to preserve goodwill

● in conjunction with your accountant and insurers, at an early stage devise a cost-effective plan to minimise any interruption to your business caused by the loss.

CHECKLIST

● Start listing your claim as soon as possible after the loss.

● Organise the preparation of your claim, and work to an orderly system.

● Keep copies of all your claim details.

● Resist any temptation to inflate your claim, or attempt to profit from it in some other way, as you risk losing everything, including your reputation.

● Make sure all alternative estimates you obtain are based on the same scope of work.

● Use insurance company 'helplines' when appropriate.

● If employing professional advisers, check their credentials and obtain estimates for any fees you have to pay.

● When completing claim forms, be truthful, brief and do not make guesses.

● Plan ahead as much as possible, to avoid unnecessary delays.

CASE STUDIES

Noah leaves everything to his secretary

Noah has an urgent business call, so he dashes off and leaves his secretary to deal with the insurance company's claims inspector. Noah's long suffering secretary, Anita, does her best to explain what happened.

The inspector informs Anita he cannot give any assurance that the costs incurred so far by Noah will be fully covered by his policy. Further, more detailed investigations would be required. Subject to his manager's approval, they will probably appoint loss adjusters to deal with the claim. In the meantime, the inspector leaves a claim form for Noah to complete.

On his return, Noah is furious to hear the news from Anita. He is not going to be messed around by some junior claims official, and will certainly not deal with a loss adjuster, as his contract is with the insurance company. He tells her to fill out the claim form for him, putting down every cost in full.

Anita does as she is told, and Noah sends off the form, without checking it properly.

Dora follows the claim procedure properly

Dora finds the specialist cleaners appointed by her insurers to be helpful. They soon have her kitchen and hallway ready for repair and redecoration.

Having confirmed there is no charge by the fire brigade for tackling the fire, Dora sets about getting three alternative builders' estimates, as requested by her buildings insurers. Her friend recommends a local contractor and she picks two others from *Yellow Pages*. One cannot undertake the work for several months, so Dora asks another contractor instead.

She completes the building section of the claim form, marking in the 'amount claimed' column, 'builders' estimates to follow'.

The contents claim seems fairly straightforward to Dora, involving replacement of a chip pan and various other kitchen utensils and crockery. She visits local shops and writes down the prices of new replacements. Where she cannot find replacements, Dora consults several mail order catalogues. The relevant prices are entered on the claim form, which she signs and posts off to the insurance company.

The next day, Dora telephones the insurance company and asks if she may purchase a few of the more essential replacement items immediately. They agree, but advise her to keep any receipts.

Ella discovers problems with her claim

Ella is passed a claim form by her brokers, who inform her of the problems with her claim:

● She was using the car for business purposes, which she did not declare in the proposal form.

● She admitted liability to the other driver, prejudicing her own insurer's position.

● She had her own care repaired without informing her insurers and obtaining their approval.

Ella fills out the claim form, answering all the questions honestly and carefully. She attaches copies of the relevant accounts.

Aware of her difficult position, Ella decides to send a letter with the claim form, explaining her errors. She points out:

● Her failure to declare business use for the car on the proposal form was simply an oversight.

● As she was in the wrong concerning the accident, she felt there was no alternative but to own up and accept the blame.

● She had repairs carried out immediately, because she was upset about her new car, and wanted to return home in it as soon as possible.

DISCUSSION POINTS

1. Discuss the fairness of the onus being placed on the insured to prepare and compile a claim at his own expense?

2. In what ways are 'new-for-old'/'reinstatement-as-new' policies not always in the best public interest?

3. Motor insurance contracts, like most other insurance contracts, are renewed on an annual basis, with insurers inviting renewal, rather than automatically reissuing the policy. What are the pros and cons of this system?

6
Submitting Your Claim

THINKING POSITIVE

A large proportion of the population happily gambles part of the weekly housekeeping on the National Lottery. Some think of insurance claims as a lottery, but the outcome of a claim should never be a gamble. It is the tangible result of an insurance contract, and should be treated in a business-like manner, with both parties seeking a fair and reasonable settlement.

Your aim should be to submit a well-documented claim to insurers, clearly set out and easy to follow. Not only will this impress insurers, but you will also gain satisfaction and confidence from doing a good job. A claim presented in this way normally leads to a swift and amicable conclusion.

The more positive your attitude is to the submission of a claim, the more positive your insurers will be in dealing with it.

ORGANISING THE PRESENTATION

If you are handling your own claim, without the services of a broker, loss assessor, or other outside agent, the first step is to set up a **claim file**, or files if more than one policy is involved. Those with computers will probably use that facility instead of, or as well as a file.

So often invoices, estimates, letters and other documents concerning a claim are scattered around the house. This gives rise to frustration, oversights and delay. Supplementary claims may have to be submitted as missing items come to light, causing annoyance to insurers and further delays.

Extra time and care taken at this stage saves twice the time later on.

When the claim simply comprises a completed claim form and attached supporting invoices or estimates, presentation and submission is a fairly straightforward affair. But if several policies are involved, with damage and losses under each, then it can become more complicated.

With most property claims of any size, rarely do all the claim details become available at the same time. Various costs tend to be submitted over a period, sometimes months or even years. The claim form and available invoices/estimates are submitted to insurers at an early stage, while others are forwarded as they are received. Organisation in these circumstances is of paramount importance, otherwise it is easy to lose control of the claim.

Keeping control of the claim

Tips for keeping control of a long-running claim are:

1. Maintain dated lists of all documents submitted to insurers, with photocopies of the documents themselves.

2. Interim payments may be received from insurers, in respect of invoices submitted. It is imperative to keep an accurate record of all payments received, and the relevant invoices.

3. Keep a schedule, so that at any time you can ascertain:

- what claim details have been submitted to you
- what claim details have been passed on to insurers
- which invoices have been the subject of payments by insurers
- which invoices remain unpaid
- what claim details are still awaited.

TIMING THE SUBMISSION OF DETAILS

Generally, there is no set time limit for the **submission of claim details** to insurers, as long as they are sent within a *reasonable* period of time.

Any undue delay could result in the insurers making deductions from your claim, to exclude any inflationary cost increases since the date of the loss.

There are certain claims where insurers expect, or even insist, on information being passed to them or some other party immediately, or within a stipulated time. For instance:

1. After a theft or attempted theft, an accidental loss, vandalism, or loss, damage or injury caused by malicious persons, it is a general policy condition that the police are notified as soon as possible.

2. In the event of a potential liability claim against you, or a member of your family living with you, you *must* inform your insurers

immediately you are aware of the incident giving rise to the claim, before the claim is received.

Other actions to take, where timing is important, are:

● give your insurers full details *in writing* as soon as possible

● without delay, send your insurers any letter, writ, summons or other legal document received in connection with the incident

● take immediate steps to prevent a recurrence of the problem (but do not dispose of any evidence relating to the cause of the incident).

3. Following a motor accident, drivers often agree to let their respective insurers deal with their own cars, or even not to claim. Soon afterwards, one driver receives a letter from the other, holding him responsible for the accident.

Any such letter (and subsequent letters) should straightaway be passed to your insurers, unanswered. Send it with your own account of the accident, and any witnesses' statements available. Be sure to keep copies.

Many people think that once their claim has been submitted, it is too late to add additional losses discovered later. This commonly happens with burglaries, where discovery of a missing item may be weeks or months after the break-in.

Insurers are generally sympathetic to these situations, and provided there is a good reason, they will accept supplementary claims.

HEADING-OFF QUERIES

When checking claims, insurance companies, loss adjusters or motor claims assessors will inevitably find points to query. These can take time to sort out, delaying claim settlement and causing frustration.

Clearly, it is to your benefit if some of these queries, many of which regularly occur, can be headed-off.

In some cases, queries arise simply due to lack of care in completing the claim form, such as omitting to sign it, or illegible writing.

To avoid unnecessary queries:

1. In completing the claim form, aim for:
   ● neatness and clear writing
   ● brief, accurate answers to the general questions
   ● detailed descriptions of the items subject of the claim.

2. If any of the property included in the claim belongs to another person, make this clear, and fully explain how it came to be in your possession. Give the name and address of the owner.

   Whether your insurers will pay this part of the loss will depend on a number of factors:
   - the terms under which you were holding the property
   - the cause of the loss or damage, and if you were negligent in relation to that cause.

If the owner has his own insurance cover on the property in question, he will be expected to claim on his own insurers, leaving the two insurance companies to sort out liability issues afterwards.

3. Household-type claim forms usually ask you to state the current rebuilding cost of buildings, and the total current replacement value of contents.

   These questions worry some policyholders, and they can insert figures which bear little resemblance to reality.

   Insurers are seeking your confirmation that your sum(s) insured is adequate. If you think your cover is adequate, insert the current sum insured in the box. If not, either reassess the value yourself, or seek outside help to arrive at a correct valuation to insert in the answer box. Never take a guess. The repercussions, both for the claim and the future, could be very costly.

4. Check the answers you give on the claim form agree with the declarations you gave on the proposal form. If there are discrepancies, give an explanation to insurers. Failure to do so could lead to a major query.

5. If your car was being driven by another driver with your permission at the time of an accident, you will have to give full details of the driver on the claim form.

   Assuming the driver has his own vehicle, he should tell his insurers about the accident. He may not be making a claim himself, but your insurers could try to involve his insurers in sharing the claim.

6. On the claim form, it is advisable to write an answer in each box, even if it has to be 'not applicable' or 'not known'. To leave an answer box blank invites a query.

7. In relation to car repairs, sort out and agree in writing any amount you have to pay for betterment, after the insurer's engineer has inspected, and before the work is carried out. To leave discussion on this until later can cause not only a query, by a major dispute.

8. Should you have personal property stolen from your car, for which you could claim either under your motor policy, your household policy or an all risks policy, make it clear to the insurers from whom you are claiming that no claim has been submitted on the other policy or policies.

KEEPING THE CLAIM MOVING

Customer care and **service standards** are the gospels preached in the modern high-technology business world. We are informed that delays and oversights are no longer acceptable to insurers, and therefore, as policyholders we should feel secure in the knowledge that once our claim is submitted, it will be processed quickly and efficiently.

Reality can paint a rather different picture. It remains as necessary as ever for us to push and prod once our claim has been submitted. Some insurers handle claims better and more speedily than others, but backlogs still occur. Our own appointed representative or advisors may also be guilty of delay. The onus is on us to make certain our particular claim keeps on the top of the pile.

You can take steps to avoid your claim from being unnecessarily delayed.

1. When submitting the claim, ask the insurance company or loss adjusters when you can expect to hear from them. Impose time limits, where practicable.

2. If you do not hear anything by the stated date, telephone and ask what is happening, and why you have not been contacted.

3. When submitting your claim, ask if there are any actions you can take to speed up matters.

4. Never give the impression time is of no importance. This is one way of ensuring your claim is kept at the bottom of the pile.

5. Avoid causing confusion, and therefore delay, by raising fresh issues concerning the claim, before other outstanding issues have been sorted out.

6. Cooperate with insurers as fully as possible, even though you may sometimes feel their questions are repetitive and irritating.

7. Answer any questions, or other points raised by insurers, without

delay (a claim may be put to one side while your answers are awaited, even though the greater part of the claim is not affected by those answers).

8. If you cannot get satisfactory service from the person handling your claim, ask to speak to their manager or supervisor.

Delays are not solely due to insurance companies or loss adjusters. Non-insurance personnel may hold up matters, unless you take action. For example, builders are notoriously slow at sending in their bills and unreliable when giving starting and finishing dates for their work. You need to be firm and persistent with such people.

Many claimants consider that, as they have paid their premiums, any claims should be dealt with by their insurance companies, without them having to do anything more. As with most things in life, it is not that simple.

An insurance claim is about deciding what level of payment of money you are entitled to under the terms of your policy. This will be your insurance company's main priority.

When it comes to the actual repair or replacement, be it a household item, a car or a business machine, you will be at the centre of any decisions or work programmes, as you would if insurance was not involved. Most claims are not finally settled until the repair or replacement has been completed.

In the circumstances, the major onus will be on you, the policyholder, to keep the claim moving, both as regards payments from insurers, and the carrying out of the agreed remedial works.

If you impress insurers, repairers, or any other involved parties with your positive attitude and efficiency, this will be reflected in their attitude to you and your claim.

CHECKLIST

● Aim to submit a well-documented claim to insurers, clearly set out and easy to follow.

● Set up a file for your claim.

● Keep control of the claim by good organisation, as documents concerning the claim are received or despatched.

● Keep lists and photocopies of all documentation sent to insurers.

- If interim payments are received from insurers, maintain an accurate record of these, and who you distribute them to.

- Avoid any undue delay in submitting claim details, which could be penalised.

- Acquaint yourself with policy time-limits for certain types of losses.

- Make certain the claim form is filled in neatly, and properly, to avoid queries and delays.

- On the claim form, give a full explanation of any unusual circumstances.

- Fill in all the answer boxes on the claim form, even if only to state 'not known', and never guess at answers.

- To keep your claim moving, immediately pass on any relevant paperwork to the insurance company.

- Where possible arrange response time limits for your insurance company or their experts, when you submit your claim, or any relevant questions.

- Keep pressure on contractors, suppliers, or other persons handling repair works to avoid unnecessary delays.

- Make sure contractors/suppliers submit invoices promptly.

CASE STUDIES

Noah agrees to meet the loss adjuster

Noah receives a telephone call from the loss adjuster, Ivor Fairdeal, requesting a meeting. Noah refuses. Ivor explains he will look at the claim impartially, and arrange a fair settlement within the policy terms. If Noah still refuses to meet him, he must inform insurers but this will lead to a delay. Noah relents, and they arrange to meet the following day.

At the meeting, Ivor questions Noah concerning the circumstances of the loss, and his actions afterwards. He then informs Noah his detailed report will be sent to insurers, highlighting the problems with the claim, on which he will need insurer's instructions. These are:

(a) On the claim form there is mention of several small previous theft claims, not declared on the proposal form.

(b) Noah had replaced some of the damaged office equipment, but the original machines might have been repairable.

While awaiting insurer's instructions Ivor will continue to check the pricing of the claim, as set down on the claim form.

Noah maintains he expects to be fully reimbursed for his outlay so far, and the remainder of the claim paid in full.

Before leaving, Ivor Fairdeal has a word with Noah's secretary Anita. She has her own 'new-for-old' household contents policy, and he advises her to claim on her own policy for the typewriter, under the 'goods temporarily removed' section. Although Noah has cover for 'employees effects', her own insurers will be able to deal with her claim more quickly, and without deductions for wear and tear. The two insurers will then sort out any contribution between themselves, which will not affect Anita in any way. She readily agrees.

Dora's claim is going well

Dora receives a telephone call from her insurance company, on receipt of her completed claim form and contents claim. They are generally satisfied with the pricing, except for several catalogue-based prices. They suggest 10 per cent deductions to these prices.

After sending the claim form, Dora discovered some additional items of damage. Plastic containers and a picnic set had melted. The claims handler informs Dora these items may be added to her claim. She should obtain replacement prices and submit them, quoting her claim reference number.

Dora also mentions that one or two of the original claim figures were too low in relation to actual replacement costs. She agrees to forward the purchase receipts.

The next day, Dora receives the three builders' estimates for the required repairs and redecoration. She takes copies, and sends the originals to her insurance company, requesting their authority to proceed, within a week.

Ella's insurers decline liability for her claim

Ella Bent receives a letter from a firm of solicitors representing the driver of the other car involved in the accident. They refer to her admission of liability, and enclose the bill for repairs to their client's car. She forwards this correspondence, unanswered, to her insurance company.

Several weeks pass without any word. Increasingly anxious, Ella asks her brokers to find out the position. She is told the matter is in the hands of underwriters, but a decision is expected within the week.

Two days later, Ella receives a letter from her insurers. They inform her that, regrettably, due to breaches of the policy conditions, they have no alternative but to decline liability, both for her claim, and that of the other driver.

DISCUSSION POINTS

1. How would the policyholder benefit if, instead of him submitting a claim, the insurance company assessed the loss and made a payment?

2. How could insurance companies improve their claims procedures?

3. Discuss the 'pros and cons' of the trend by insurance companies to set up their own vehicle repair centres, and how is this likely to affect claims?

7
Dealing With Your Insurance Company

THINKING POSITIVE

The thought of having to deal with a large insurance company, or even their appointed loss adjuster, fills many people with dread. 'I'm frightened of wasting their time', or 'They'll think I'm stupid if I ask that', are expressions commonly encountered.

You should never feel this way. Insurance company offices are staffed by ordinary people, often working under great pressure. In relation to claims, they usually want to reach a settlement with you as quickly and amicably as possible.

If you have any questions or queries, no matter how trivial they may seem, take a positive stance and ask them. As with any problem in life, it will only be resolved once it is brought out into the open. Claims officials are there for that purpose, and they have probably heard the same questions or queries before.

Insurance is a service industry, and insurance companies are there to *serve* their policyholders in their time of need. *That is why you pay your premiums.*

RECORDING CONTACTS

No matter how straightforward your claim may seem at the outset, things can go wrong. Personnel changes at the insurance company, mail going astray, wrong decisions or incompetence are factors which may complicate a claim at some stage.

Similar type problems can affect the insurance claim repair work, occasionally leading to legal action. A contractor may cease trading part way through the repair contract, or the work itself is unsatisfactory. Although the insurance company may be providing the funds, you are usually the employer for the works, and you will be left to sort out matters.

Admittedly, such setbacks are not experienced by the majority of people making claims, but they happen, and you need to protect your position by taking certain precautions from the start of the claim process.

Logging telephone calls

● In your claim file keep a log in chronological order, of all telephone calls relating to the claim.

● Record the date, time and length of call, and of course, the name of the other person.

● Alongside this basic data, briefly record the main points of the conversation, but try to set down word for word any important statements or decisions.

● Ask the other person to confirm the telephone conversation in writing, if any major issues are discussed.

Filing correspondence

● Any correspondence concerning the claim, or the remedial work, should be filed in chronological order, with copies of all forms, letters or cheques you may send.

● On correspondence received, mark the date it arrived (some letters arrive a week or more after the date shown on them).

● If unhappy with the content of a letter from your insurance company, or some other party, telephone them straight away to make your point, and confirm in writing.

● Before filing any item of paperwork, make sure it is not necessary to send it (or a copy) to some other person or company.

Playing the name game

People are notoriously bad at remembering names, even though they may have a photographic memory for faces.

During the course of a claim, particularly a large or complicated one, it is likely you will meet or speak to a number of people at the insurance company, and others associated with the replacements or repairs.

● Establish and record the name of any person you meet concerning the claim.

● If appropriate, ask for a business card.

- Ascertain his precise role in the matter, if he it not present at your request.

- If you attend a meeting about the claim, record the names (and the names of their companies), of all those present.

CONFIRMING DISCUSSIONS AND ACTIONS

As well as recording contacts relating to your claim, it is also important to keep **written confirmation** of discussions and any actions taken.

In the event of future difficulties, such confirmation of what has taken place at each stage will prove invaluable. But even if there are no problems, the written record is a useful *aide memoire*.

The sort of information or actions which should be confirmed in writing are:

- insurer's decision that your policy covers the loss
- if insurers decline to deal with your claim, or any part of it, the reasons why
- any actions you are expected to take
- decisions concerning the carrying out of the remedial work, or parts of the work
- all estimated costs relevant to the claim
- the extent of any contribution you are expected to make towards repair/replacement costs
- for theft claims, you should get a letter from the police confirming what has been reported as stolen
- priced details of any extra repair work found necessary should be confirmed to all interested parties
- the content and outcome of any meetings in connection with the claim

ADDRESSING PROBLEMS

Problems rarely go away. If not dealt with, they fester and become even greater problems.

By reference to the Insurance Ombudsman's report for 1995, it is clear from the summary of cases completed that year, the greatest problem areas include:

Household buildings and contents

- disputes over policy terms

- failure of initial proof
- communication difficulties, administrative failure and poor service.

Motor

- disputes over policy terms
- disagreements over under-insurance and value
- communication difficulties, administrative failure and poor service.

Whether you are faced with these or other problem areas, there has to be a final outcome. So why not do your best to arrive at that stage sooner, rather than later. After all, the longer the claim is outstanding, the longer you are out of pocket.

Where a more technical problem is involved, such as a dispute over policy terms, or disagreement over under-insurance and value, address the matter by getting early expert advice. If you use a broker or insurance consultant, he should be able to help.

Otherwise, have a word with an outside agency, like the Citizen's Advice Bureau.

Of course, you always have the right to engage the services of a solicitor, valuer, engineer or other professional, but you have to pay their fees.

Seeing the manager

Once you have obtained evidence to support your case, telephone or write to your insurance company, and ask for a meeting with the claims manager, or the branch manager. Do not let yourself be talked into seeing a junior claims person.

Present your case to the manager as clearly and concisely as you can. You should receive a fair hearing, but that does not mean you will necessarily hear the decision you want.

Normally, at such meetings, views will be aired by both sides, and the manager will then look into your case with those members of his staff concerned, before writing to you with his decision.

Considering other options

Should you still feel dissatisfied with the outcome, it might be worthwhile discussing the problems with the Association of British Insurer's representative in your area. The Association represents about 430 insurance companies, which between them account for over 90 per cent of the business of UK insurance companies. Their headquarters at 51 Gresham Street, London EC2V 7HQ will put you in touch with a local representative.

If you remain unhappy with your treatment, you should write to the chief general manager of your insurance company, setting out your case to him. This is the ultimate step in trying to resolve a problem within the insurance company framework.

Complaining about service

Complaints concerning communication difficulties, administrative failure or poor service, can normally be resolved with the insurance company, without having to consult outside agencies. Any allegation of this kind will receive serious and sympathetic consideration by insurers, anxious to promote **service standards**.

To address such a problem, follow the same steps as for those of a more technical nature. Because the eventual payment from your insurer may not be affected, there can be a tendency to let a service complaint drop after a short while, even if you still believe your complaint is justified. *Do not be deflected.* In return for your premium, you are entitled to good service, as well as a fair claim settlement.

Insurers should deal with our claims, and problems concerning claims, in a fair, courteous and efficient manner. In return, they are entitled to expect us to be honest and reasonable. If problems are addressed in this way by both parties, then the majority will be sorted out quickly and amicably.

PREVENTING DELAYS

The claims side of the insurance business is 'booming'. This is particularly so in motor claims, as car ownership and usage steadily increases, especially amongst young people.

Introducing new systems

Insurance companies have tried to offset the extra work by greater efficiency, with claims departments taking advantage of sophisticated computer systems, and added emphasis has been placed on telephone skills.

In the case of motor claims, insurers strive to provide a comprehensive accident management service to the customer. In addition to organising repairs, insurers offer **roadside assistance, vehicle recovery, a temporary vehicle, uninsured loss recovery** and many other related services. Their aim is to provide this level of quality service without delay.

For household claims, insurers have favoured a similar strategy, by providing an active response to early claim notification by customers. More claims are being settled by fast-tracking methods, with insurers offering replacement goods from specialist suppliers (so exploiting their vast buying power and making a cost saving for themselves).

Despite these innovative changes, delays remain a major source of dissatisfaction amongst policyholders. So far, the main beneficiaries of the new technology and systems have been the insurance companies, with increased productivity and reduced claim costs.

Taking action

As a policyholder, what can you do to try to prevent your claim being delayed?

The tried and tested strategy over the years has been to chase and hassle the insurance company at every opportunity. You become such a nuisance, they will give you what you want, if only to get rid of you.

Most people prefer to act in a more civilised and pleasant way, even when angry over delay. For this section of the insuring public, there are a number of steps you can take:

1. Do not be guilty of delay yourself. To chase the insurance company, and find they are waiting for you to do something does not help your cause.

2. Do not be fobbed off by such excuses as 'I'm waiting for my supervisor to look at the file', or 'The computer went down on Wednesday'. Insist on prompt attention to your claim, and ask the claims handler when you should call back for a decision.

3. If you cannot get a satisfactory reply from the claims handler, ask to speak to the supervisor.

4. Should your insurance be arranged through an outside agency, such as a broker or building society, get them to put pressure on the insurance company.

5. Many insurance companies market their products promising 'instant claims service', or 'we guarantee to deal with all your claims promptly'. Refer such promises back to an insurer, in the event of their delay.

6. Ask your insurance company if there is anything you can do to speed up matters.

7. Diary all calls/letters when chasing up your claim. If the delay continues, write to the manager of the insurance company, setting out the times and dates of your previous attempts to get satisfaction. Demand a reply by return.

ARRANGING PAYMENTS UNDER POLICY

At the start of the claim procedure, discuss and agree the method of payment to be adopted by insurers when settling the claim. There are various options which are listed below under the relevant policies.

Household and business policies

● Payment can be made directly to you, against estimates, or more likely against invoices.

● With your approval, direct payment can be made to your contractor, supplier or service provider.

● If your house is mortgaged to a building society or bank, their interest will be noted on the policy, and any payments are likely to be sent to them (they will release the monies to you after inspecting the completed works).

● Where your insurer has elected to reinstate or replace, instead of making a cash payment under the policy, the insurer is wholly responsible for paying the contractor or supplier.

● If a claim is likely to be outstanding for a long while, insurers will make certain interim stage payments to you, where costs have been incurred and invoices received.

Motor policies

● After your car has been satisfactorily repaired, the repairer will be paid direct, leaving you to pay any extra sums for which you are liable.

● If you have already paid the repairer, your insurers will forward a cheque for their agreed proportion to you.

● Should your car be uneconomic to repair, and classed as a 'total loss', you will be offered a cash settlement.

● For a broken windscreen, which you can usually have replaced without first checking with insurers using their recommended firm, they normally pay the repairer direct.

● In the event of your car being stolen and not recovered, insurers will offer you a payment on a 'total loss' basis. (You are not bound to take back the car and return the insurance monies if your car is subsequently found.)

CHECKLIST

● Log all telephone calls.

● Record names of all persons (and their firms), you meet concerning your claim.

● Confirm in writing any discussions, or actions taken, in connection with the claim, or associated remedial work.

● File all correspondence in chronological order, with copies of any forms, letters, cheques or other documents.

● Mark the date received on incoming letters or other documents.

● Make sure you have acted on any letters received before filing them.

● Act positively and swiftly regarding any problems which arise, seeking professional advice where necessary.

● Refuse to accept any unjustified delays by your insurers.

● Take any complaint you may have with your insurance company to a higher level within the company.

● At the outset, discuss and agree the method of claim payment to be adopted by your insurers.

CASE STUDIES

Noah decides to seek legal advice

Noah is contacted by the loss adjuster, Ivor, who has received insurer's instructions.

As regards the non-disclosure on the proposal form of the previous small theft claims, insurers accept this was an oversight, and not deliberate concealment. They are prepared to overlook it, particularly as there is no direct relevance to the present claim.

However, if insurers had known of these claims the premium would have been slightly higher. They expect Noah to pay the extra amount of premium.

As for Noah replacing the damaged office machines, insurers consider their liability to be restricted to the cost of repairs only, where repair is economic. Ivor is to establish the relevant repair costs.

Noah is unhappy and intends to have a word with his solicitor. Ivor says he will confirm the position in writing.

Dora remembers to ask for written confirmation

Dora waits for her insurance company to contact her, but a week passes with no news. She telephones the company and speaks to Sharon, the claims handler dealing with her claim.

Sharon apologises for the delay with Dora's claim, but she will find the papers and telephone Dora later that day.

By the next morning, Dora is angry, as she has not been contacted by her insurers. She telephones them again, only to discover Sharon is taking a day's leave. She asks to speak to the claims manager, who introduces himself as Gerry.

He listens to Dora's story and after apologising for the delays promises to sort out something that morning.

Later that day Dora hears from her insurers that she may proceed with the building repairs and redecoration, based on the lowest of the three estimates, from Bodgett & Scram. Dora is asked to instruct the contractors, and on completion of the work, submit their bill to the insurers. They will then send Dora a cheque, so that she may pay the contractors.

As for the contents claim, one of their claims inspectors will call on her within the week to discuss a settlement.

Dora asks her insurers to confirm the conversation in writing.

Bodgett & Scram agree to start the works the following Monday and complete in ten days.

Ella is left with substantial costs to pay

Ella, on receipt of her insurers's letter declining liability, decides to seek legal advice from her solicitors.

They advise that insurers are within their rights to repudiate liability, having regard to the breach of policy conditions. However, the solicitors offer to contact the insurers on Ella's behalf, to find out if they might be prepared to reverse their decision. Their efforts prove unsuccessful.

Ella, left facing substantial costs, ponders her next move. As her insurers are members of The Insurance Ombudsman's Bureau, she explores the possibility of pursuing her claim in that direction. Meanwhile, she comes under increasing pressure from the other motorist's solicitors to meet his £600 claim. Legal proceedings are threatened.

DISCUSSION POINTS

1. Insurers are under a duty to deal with their policyholders' claims on a 'fair and reasonable' basis. What do you understand by the term 'fair and reasonable'?

2. With motor policies it is common to find a 'new car' clause. If your car is stolen and not recovered, or is damaged beyond economic repair within one year of its first registration as new in your name, insurers will replace your car with a new car of the same make, model and specification, if immediately available in the UK. How would you approach insurers if there is no replacement model available?

3. Insurance companies would benefit from having greater dialogue with consumer advice organisations, especially on the technicalities of insurance. Discuss how this suggestion could help individual policyholders, with particular reference to the processing of claims.

8
Negotiating a Settlement

THINKING POSITIVE

Everybody hears of other peoples' bad experiences with insurance companies, and of course, some of us will have had our own skirmishes. The popular concept is of a solitary figure taking on this huge, largely faceless, powerful organisation.

Insurance companies are generally fair-minded, but as with every business, you will encounter the occasional maverick employee. The key to a successful claim negotiation comes down to your good planning, preparation and presentation.

Finally, when negotiations end, *you* will have to decide whether to accept or refuse a settlement offer. You may seek *advice* from others, but always make your own decisions.

When negotiating your claim settlement:

* be prepared
* be calm
* be patient
* be determined
* above all, be successful.

AGREEING THE BASIS OF SETTLEMENT

The amount payable under the policy is dependent on the following factors.

Household insurances (buildings)

* Whether you have a **reinstatement-as-new policy**, which should pay the full cost of repairs or rebuilding, provided the sum insured is adequate.

* If you have an **indemnity policy**, a **reinstatement-as-new policy**

116

Part A - Buildings

Important

Part A of your policy only applies if *you* have chosen to insure your *buildings* and the word *'Buildings'* appears on your latest *schedule*.

You are covered by the insurance provided under Part A during the *period of insurance*. However, this depends on the limits and Special *Exclusions* (shown in Part A), General *Exclusions* (see page 35) and General Conditions (see pages 36 and 37).

Claims settlement

We can choose to

1 pay the cost of work carried out to rebuild, replace or repair your *buildings*; or

2 arrange for your *buildings* to be rebuilt, replaced or repaired; or

3 pay *you* cash based on our estimate of the cost to rebuild, replace or repair your *buildings*; or if *you* choose not to rebuild or repair your *buildings we* can choose to

4 pay the difference between the market value of the *buildings* immediately before the loss or damage happened and the market value of the *buildings* immediately after the loss or damage happened. However, this must not be more than the cost to rebuild or repair the *buildings*

for any loss or damage as a result of any of the circumstances listed on pages 11, 12 and 13.

If at the time of loss or damage, the *amount insured* for your *buildings* is less than the cost of rebuilding them as new, *we* will only pay the following fraction of any claim that *we* accept

Amount insured
_____
Rebuilding cost.

For example, if the *amount insured* is only three quarters of the total rebuilding cost, *we* will only pay three quarters of the claim.

We will not pay any extra cost for extending or improving your *buildings* once they are rebuilt as new.

We will not pay for the cost of altering or replacing any items or parts of items which are not lost or damaged and which form part of a set, suite or other article, of the same type, colour or design.

Fig. 12. Household policy claim settlement wording, incorporating 'average clause'

with an inadequate sum insured, or you do not intend to reinstate the damage, then the payment will be based on the cost of repairs or rebuilding, less deductions for wear and tear. The deductions will vary according to the expected lifespan and condition of the item in question. For instance, stone walls have an almost limitless life and any wear and tear element would be negligible. But electric wiring or decorations have limited lifespans, so sizeable deductions could be required.

● Should you elect *not* to rebuild or repair after damage, insurers usually reserve the option to pay the difference between the market value of buildings prior to the loss or damage, and the market value of the buildings following the loss or damage. This can work out substantially less than the repair/rebuilding cost. In any event, the maximum sum payable is:
(a)   the cost of rebuilding or repairing your buildings, or
(b)   the amount insured for buildings
whichever is the less. (see Figure 12 which shows a household policy claim settlement wording, incorporating an average clause.)

Although terms vary between different insurers' policies, the following commonly found clauses will influence the amount payable under your policy:

(a)   matching items (such as bathroom suites) – insurers will not pay for undamaged items forming part of a matching suite or set.

(b)   policy excess – where you have to pay the first part of a claim, this will be deducted by insurers when making payment.

(c)   alternative accommodation/loss of rent – if you have to take temporary accommodation due to your home being uninhabitable due to insured damage, or you lose rent due to you, this is insured, subject to a limit, normally 10 per cent of your buildings sum insured (any sum payable under this section is additional to the sum insured on buildings in the event of a total loss).

Household insurances (contents)

Factors governing the amount payable under a contents policy are similar to those mentioned for buildings.

The three main types of cover offered by insurers are:

● replacement-as-new (new-for-old)

5 CLAIM SETTLEMENT FOR COVER 2

Provided the loss or damage is covered under **Your Policy**, **We** will settle **Your** claim as explained below, subject to the maximum amount payable.

1 a Where the damage can be economically repaired, **We** will either arrange or authorise repair
   b Where the damaged or lost item can be replaced with an item of similar quality, **We** will either arrange or authorise replacement. If an exact replacement is not available, **We** will either arrange or authorise replacement with an item of similar quality
   c Where **We** are unable to economically repair or replace the item with an item of similar quality, **We** will make a cash payment equal to an agreed replacement value
   d Where we have offered repair or replacement but **You** prefer a cash settlement, **We** will pay **You** an amount equal to the amount **We** would have paid had the item been repaired or replaced
2 For clothing and household linen **We** may make a deduction for wear, tear and depreciation
3 If the **Sum Insured** is less than the cost of replacing all the **Contents** as new, **We** may make a deduction for wear, tear and depreciation on all items

Maximum Amount Payable
The maximum amount payable in respect of any one incident is:

1 **Contents**	— the **Sum Insured** (less any **Excess**) subject to the following limits unless **Your Schedule** shows an increased amount
i **Valuables** in total	£10,000 or one third of the **Sum Insured** for **Contents** whichever is the greater
ii Any one **Valuable**	£1,000
iii **Business Equipment**	£3,000
iv **Money**	£250
v Satellite aerials	£250
vi Visitors' Personal Possessions	£250
vii Replacement Locks	£250
viii Documents	£250
2 **Contents** in the Garden	— The amount payable will be the lower of £250 or the amount shown in paragraphs i-iv above
3 Theft of **Contents** in domestic outbuildings, garages or greenhouses	— The amount payable will be the lower of £2,000 or the amount shown in paragraphs i-iv
4 Alternative Accommodation	— 20% of the **Sum Insured** on **Contents**

The **Sum Insured** on **Contents** will not be reduced following payment of a claim

THE CONDITIONS AND EXCLUSIONS WHICH APPLY TO YOUR WHOLE POLICY ARE SHOWN ON PAGES 32-34

Fig. 13. Common basis of claim settlement policy wording (contents).

- indemnity
- limited new-for-old.

1. **Replacement-as-new-policies** pay the full cost of replacement for loss or total destruction of items, or the cost of repairing those damaged. Usually, deductions for wear and tear apply to clothing and linen. The whole claim could be subject to deductions for wear and tear if the sum insured is low on a replacement-as-new basis, or you do not intend to replace or repair the damaged item(s).

2. For indemnity policies, deductions for wear and tear apply to all affected items, where appropriate.

3. Limited new-for-old insurance on contents is selected where a policyholder is looking for replacement-as-new cover on newer items in the home, typically less than five years old, but is prepared to have lesser indemnity cover on older items. Again, indemnity only is payable on all items, if the sum insured is inadequate or you do not intend to repair or replace.

   Figure 13 illustrates a common basis of a claim settlement policy wording for household contents.
   Other clauses found in contents policies which affect the sum payable are:

- *Matching items* (such as 3 piece suites) – insurers will not pay for undamaged parts of a matching suite or set.

- *Policy excess* – this will be deducted by insurers when making payment.

- *Alternative accommodation and/or loss of rent* – as with buildings policies, insurers will pay the reasonable cost of your alternative accommodation, or pay any loss of rent payable either to you or by you. The sum payable is limited to 10 per cent, or possibly 20 per cent of your contents sum insured.

- *For high risk items*, like jewellery, television, videos, stereos, there is usually an overall payment limit, perhaps £7,500, with a single article limit of say £1,000.

- *Where keys to your home are stolen*, the cost of replacing external door locks will be paid by insurers, subject to a cost limit of say £250.

- *Personal money is covered*, but limited to a maximum payment by insurers of perhaps £250.

- *Your legal liability for credit*, debit, charge, cheque or cash cards is usually insured by a contents policy, but subject to a limit of about £500.

- *Fatal accidents* – most policies include provision for a payment, often £5,000, if you or your spouse suffer fatal injury due to accident, assault or fire in the home, accident while travelling on public transport, or assault in the street.

- *If you are a tenant*, most policies include cover for your legal liability as tenant, for damage by an insured event to your home. The sum payable is limited to 10% of your contents sum insured.

Motor insurance

The basis for settling an own-vehicle motor insurance claim is relatively simple, but having said that, the process is a constant source of dissatisfaction.

Settlement is based on a repairer's estimate and subsequent invoice, after completion of the repairs. Alternatively, if your car is beyond economic repair, you will be offered a total loss settlement by insurers, based on the current market price of the car in its pre-accident condition.

Many motorists, especially men, enjoy a love affair with cars. The value of their car is much more than any book figure, and they are always going to feel discontent with the claim settlement figure.

The settlement basis can be influenced by various factors, such as:

1. *Betterment* – you may be asked to contribute towards the repair cost if replacement parts result in your car being better than before the accident. Perhaps parts were rusted, worn or previously damaged.

   You should only be asked to contribute towards such parts as the battery, exhaust system or tyres. Resist any suggestion of contribution towards bodywork repair costs, if the total cost is within the market value of the car. Generally, a vehicle will not be enhanced in value after repairs.

2. *No-claims discount (NCD)* – chiefly used in motor insurance, this is a deduction from a premium on renewal where there has been no claim in the previous year(s). Usually, this amounts to a reduction of 30 per cent on your premium in the first year, rising in annual steps to a maximum of 60 to 70 per cent.

Should you make a claim, your no claims discount will be reduced or disallowed. If you have built up a higher rate of discount, most insurers will normally only reduce it by two years step back, rather than disallowing it entirely.

Many offer a protected no claims discount, where you may pay a small fee, so that your discount will not be affected by an accident, unless you have exceeded the amount of claims allowed by the policy. This is typically two accidents in three, four or five years. In effect, you are paying an extra premium to protect your original premium.

3. *Knock-for-Knock* – your insurance company might operate a knock-for-knock agreement with the insurers of the other vehicle involved in an accident, although they are now less common. This means that each pays for the damage to the car it insures, provided the two cars are insured on a comprehensive basis. This agreement operates regardless of liability or blame.

    If liability clearly rested with the other party and can be proven, your NCD should be safe, but otherwise, it will be reduced.

4. *Even with comprehensive cover*, there could be some expenses not insured by your policy. Examples may include:

● the amount of any policy excess
● out-of-pocket expenses
● treatment or transport costs after injury
● compensation for personal injury
● loss of earnings from your workplace, due to having time off
● cost of alternative transport to work, or car hire.

If the accident was the other driver's fault, send your claim for un/insured losses direct to him by recorded delivery.

Business insurance

The basis of claim settlements for business policies is much the same as for household policies. The two common types of cover are:

1. **replacement-as-new** (no deductions for wear and tear).

2. **indemnity** (with deductions for wear and tear).

The major difference is that nearly all business policies contain an **average** or **under-insurance** clause. This means you only receive a part

E   CLAIMS SETTLEMENT

Following Damage the Insurers will pay the cost of reinstating the Property equal to its condition when new provided that

1   this is carried out without delay and in the most economical manner

2   when any Property is partially damaged the Insurers' liability shall not exceed the reinstatement cost that would have been incurred had it been wholly destroyed

3   no payment will be made until reinstatement has been carried out

4   if the damaged Property is not reinstated a loss will be settled after allowance for depreciation

5   in respect of Business Files the Insurers' liability shall be limited to costs and expenses incurred in reproducing or recompiling them but shall not include the value to the Insured of the information that they contain

Underinsurance

If at the time of Damage the total of the Sums Insured on Business Equipment specified in Schedule 1 is less than 85% of the total reinstatement cost of such Property the Insurers shall bear only that proportion of any Damage to Business Equipment which the total of the Sums Insured on Business Equipment bear to the total reinstatement cost of such Property

Automatic Reinstatement of Sums Insured

In the event of a loss the Sums Insured in Schedule 1 will be automatically reinstated by the amount of the loss provided that

1   the Insured pays the appropriate additional premium for such reinstatement of Sums Insured

2   the Insured implements without delay any amendments to the protections of the Premises that the Insurers may require

3   in respect of Damage by theft or attempted theft the automatic reinstatement of Sums Insured shall apply on the first occasion only in one Period of Insurance

Fig. 14. Typical business policy provisions for reinstatement-as-new settlement.

123

of the agreed total settlement figure if you are under-insured. The amount by which the settlement figure is reduced will be proportionate to the degree of under-insurance. For example:

Agreed cost of repairs	=	£ 1,000.00
Sum insured	=	£20,000.00
Value of property insured	=	£40,000.00
Insurers will pay:		

$$\frac{£20,000.00}{£40,000.00} \times £1,000.00 \quad = \quad £ \ 500.00$$

Figure 14 illustrates the typical business policy provisions for a reinstatement-as-new settlement.

Some other relevant points are:

●   Excesses on business policies are often higher than those on household policies.

●   Subsidence cover is usually excluded, should you have a commercial type buildings policy.

●   Should you have **all risks** cover on any valuable machines or equipment, this gives wide cover for physical loss or damage, but does *not* cover risks such as war, nuclear contamination or wear and tear.

Consequential loss (business interruption)

This type of insurance cover is for a set period after a loss, known as the indemnity period, usually a minimum of twelve months. As well as covering any loss of revenues, income or fees after disruption to your business by an insured event such as fire, the policy also covers additional expenditure reasonably incurred by you to keep the business in operation. This expenditure might include such costs as hiring and fitting out temporary premises, increased lighting and heating, or moving costs.

The basis of settlement is calculated by reference to your daily, weekly or monthly income and expenditure records, and the audited accounts for your business, particularly those for the last complete financial year before the loss.

In practice, much of the information for working out a consequential loss claim will be provided by your accountant. His fees for supplying this information are generally covered by policies.

DEALING WITH OFFERS

Some claims are paid in full without query. In other cases, the sum payable may be fixed before a claim arises, as with **valued policies** on jewellery, where a jeweller's valuation is accepted as a basis for settlement in the event of loss. However, in most claims, settlements have to be negotiated. The policyholder makes the claim, the insurer comes back with an offer, and final settlement is then negotiated.

With smaller claims in particular, insurance companies are anxious to minimise their processing costs, and have adopted various **fast-tracking** systems. So there is pressure on claims handlers, whether they be insurance company personnel or loss adjusters, to settle claims rapidly.

Whatever the size of your claim, do not be pressurised into accepting an offer you are not convinced is fair. Carefully weigh up any offer received, in your own time, and seek other advice if necessary.

If you receive an offer and you consider your claim has been scaled down unfairly, ask why. You have a right to a detailed explanation.

Motor claims

Motor insurance claims are notoriously difficult when it comes to the settlement stage, especially where the vehicle is a write-off. The insurance company's valuation and offer often falls below expectations.

If unhappy with the settlement offer, the onus will be on you to prove the car is worth more. Possibly, a report from an independent assessor may help to challenge the offer. The Institute of Automotive Engineer Assessors at Mansell House, 22 Bore Street, Lichfield, Staffs, WS13 6LP (Tel: 01543 251346) should be able to put you in touch with an assessor in your area.

General tips

In relation to settlement offers received from insurance companies, note the following:

● Never give a hasty response, even if the offer sounds good, but examine the basis of the offer in detail.

● Do not assume the information on which the insurance company's offer is based is necessarily correct.

● Be wary of accepting a settlement offer based on the cheapest quotation received, when this quotation is much lower than others.

● If an item is excluded from your claim because it should be referred to another insurer, check with that other insurer before agreeing anything.

● Do not be persuaded to accept a replacement item instead of a cash settlement, where an identical replacement is not obtainable, and you are not happy with the suggested replacement.

● Remember that any error in your policy, or ambiguity over the meaning of words or phrases is the sole responsibility of your insurers, as they drew up the document.

ARRANGING CLAIM PAYMENTS

When taking out insurance, we enter into a contract with the insurance company of our choice. In consideration of the policyholder paying the required premium, insurers agree to **indemnify** (compensate) the policyholder in the event of loss or damage to the insured property by an insured event.

Exercising the replacement option

Insurers have the option to indemnify their policyholder by replacing the lost or damaged property, instead of paying a sum of money. In practice, this option is rarely exercised for buildings or commercial losses, because:

● Insurers are reluctant to incur the cost of handling the reinstatement works.

● Any defects in the work, or other similar type problems would be insurer's responsibility.

● The cost of the remedial work would have to be fully met by insurers, even if it exceeded the sum insured.

The option is sometimes exercised if insurers are suspicious about a claim, but cannot repudiate liability due to lack of evidence. In this way, the policyholder does not receive a cash payment, defeating any attempted fraud.

But the replacement option is being increasingly taken up by insurers for contents claims. It has the following benefits for them:

● it combats possible fraudulent claims
● by using one supplier, they can obtain sizeable discounts on goods supplied (particularly electrical items and jewellery).

Insurers sell this concept to policyholders, by emphasising the speedy replacement of items, often delivered direct to the home by suppliers. In theory it sounds fine, but the scheme does not always result in customer satisfaction.

When an insurance company gives instructions for work, or places an order with their selected supplier for replacement goods, they are entirely responsible for payment of relevant invoices.

Paying the claim in cash

Most claims are still settled by insurers making a monetary payment, based on the value of the loss or damage. Under the terms of the insurance contract, insurers are obliged to draw payment cheques in the name(s) of the insured(s) shown in the policy.

For insurers to send a payment cheque to some other party, they require a **written authority (mandate)** from *all* the named insured(s) on the policy. If a building society, or bank or other such body has an interest noted on the policy, their approval will also be needed.

Claim payments direct to other parties can occur:

- when contractors or suppliers insist on direct payment by insurers, to be sure of getting their money
- if you do not want the money to go into your bank account
- where speedy payment to a contractor or supplier is necessary (it avoids you having to bank the insurer's cheque, and wait for it to be cleared before you pass on the payment)
- if you do not wish to be involved in the payment chain, acting as a 'post office' between insurers and the parties requiring payment
- should you be away while the repair contract is underway.

KNOWING YOUR RIGHTS CONCERNING PAYMENT

In relation to insurance claim payments you have certain rights, but insurance companies are often prepared to adopt other procedures, even though they are not written in the policy and you have no right to demand them.

Additional procedures of this type include:

- the making of **interim payments**, otherwise known as **payments on account**, as the claim proceeds
- where a large excess applies (such as £1,000 for subsidence damage), insurers will waive its deduction until a later stage of the claim.

As regards your rights concerning payments:

1. You have a **right of confidentiality**, and insurers should not divulge details to anyone, other than those parties named in the policy.

2. In the case of an **indemnity settlement**, the insurance monies are yours, to do with as you wish. You are not bound to repair or replace the lost/damaged items.

3. After a **theft claim** has been paid, your stolen car or other goods may be recovered by the police. You do not have to repay the insurance monies, but if you wish, you can negotiate with insurers to buy back the recovered property.

4. If your name appears as an insured on the policy, insurers cannot ignore this, even if you no longer have an interest in the insured property. Your written authority would be needed before insurers could issue a cheque not bearing your name. (This causes frequent problems with divorced couples, where the original policy has not been updated.)

CHECKLIST

● Prepare for claim negotiations by good planning, preparation and presentation.

● Understand the basis being adopted for settlement of your claim.

● When negotiating household building claim settlements, review the type of cover in force, and other relevant features, such as policy excesses or loss of rent.

● For household contents, familiarise yourself with the basis of cover you have, and the policy clauses or limits which will influence the sum payable.

● In motor insurance settlement negotiations, have particular regard to the questions of betterment and no claims discounts.

● For business insurance claims, be aware of the 'average' clause and its effect on the settlement figure.

● If a consequential loss claim is involved, introduce your accountant at an early stage, as he will understand the claim procedure, and can supply the required information.

● Treat any reduced settlement offers with caution, and ask why your claim has been scaled down.

● Should you want your business to pay another party direct, this can usually be arranged if you sign a written authority to that effect.

● After a payment is made under your policy for theft, you cannot be forced to repay those monies, should the missing property later be recovered.

CASE STUDIES

Noah threatens to change insurance companies

Noah receives written confirmation from the loss adjuster, Ivor, of the proposed basis of settlement. With the letter is an estimate, for the 'notional' cost of repairs to Noah's damaged machines of £750, against the amount of £1,950 paid by Noah for replacements.

Ivor adds that his enquiries indicate Noah's sum insured of £2,000 on office contents is low and should be £3,000. Therefore, the policy average clause operates as follows:

$$\frac{£2,000 \text{ (sum insured)}}{£3,000 \text{ (value at risk)}} \times £900 \text{ (adjusted loss)} = £600$$

Reference is also made to other aspects of Noah's claim:

1. Insurers were unhappy at the delay in reporting the loss, but they have decided to overlook that issue on this occasion.

2. Ivor will contact Noah's household insurers to sort out any contribution by the business insurers towards their outlay. He will also discuss contribution with Anita Filer's household contents insurers, who paid for her replacement typewriter.

3. There were several discrepancies between the purchase prices for the new machines shown in the claim form, and those on the invoices. However, this is irrelevant in view of the basis of settlement adopted.

4. As Noah's business is registered for VAT, no VAT is payable by insurers, as this tax can be recovered by Noah through his VAT account.

5. The extra cost incurred, over and above the normal rate, for the urgent redrawing of the ruined drawings, is outside the scope of the

policy cover, as Noah does not have consequential loss (loss of profits) insurance.

Noah decides not to incur solicitor's costs and instead, writes a letter of complaint to the head office of his insurance company. He emphasises they are being unhelpful to his new business, and if they do not meet his claim in full, he will change to another insurance company.

Dora's neighbours claim against her for damage to their kitchen

Dora arranges a meeting with the claims inspector to go through her contents claim.

Before the meeting takes place, Dora receives a shock when a letter arrives in the post from solicitors representing her new neighbour. The letter states a claim is to be made against her for smoke damage to her neighbour's kitchen. The estimated redecoration cost is £200.

Dora shows the letter to the claims inspector. He tells her not to worry, as her policy provides liability cover, in her capacity as owner/occupier of the house. Insurers will contact the neighbour's solicitors and deal with the matter, and Dora should not get involved. Any further correspondence should be passed onto her insurers, unanswered.

Due to the cause of the fire, the inspector feels Dora may have a liability, as leaving the chip pan unattended could be construed as negligence.

As regards Dora's contents claim, after going through the details with the inspector she reaches agreement, including a 10 per cent deductions on those articles priced from catalogues. Upward adjustments were needed to those prices which Dora has underestimated on the claim form, and to include the extra items omitted from the original claim.

The agreed settlement figure is £400, to which several outstanding dry-cleaning costs have to be added. The inspector promises to arrange an interim payment on account to Dora of £400, pending receipt of the dry-cleaning bill.

Ella opts for arbitration

Ella, under pressure from the other driver's solicitors, decides to pay the £600 for repairs to the other vehicle out of her own pocket.

As regards the Insurance Ombudsman, she discovers her insurance company is not a member of The Insurance Ombudsman Bureau. However, she is advised by a friend to seek advice from the Consumer Information Department of the Association of British Insures (ABI) in London. They put her in touch with their nearest regional office.

The ABI representative readily agrees to meet Ella to discuss her problem. He promises to have a word with her insurers, to discuss their decisions, but his view is that she is in a difficult position.

A few days later, Ella receives a call from the ABI representative informing her that he has spoken to her insurers, who reaffirmed that their original decision stands, for the reasons previously given to Ella. However, as they are members of the Personal Insurance Arbitration Service (PIAS), she could take her case to arbitration, or alternatively to court.

A court case would be costly, but the PIAS scheme offers a simple method of resolving a dispute by arbitration (normally on documents only), with the cost being met by insurers.

Ella opts for arbitration and writes to her insurance company to initiate the action.

DISCUSSION POINTS

1. Many claims are exaggerated by policyholders. Discuss the case for insurers regarding this as fraud, and repudiating liability for the whole claim.

2. Consider the various methods available of establishing the market value of a written-off or stolen car for the purposes of a claim settlement. Why do you think insurers are reluctant to specify a precise method of valuation in policies, such as a particular standard trade guide?

3. What are the merits of the 'average condition' in commercial policies, whereby a policyholder is self-insured in proportion to the degree of any under-insurance?

9
Handling Disputes

THINKING POSITIVE

Insurance is a subject we grumble about, almost as much as the weather. Having to pay money for protection against the effects of some disaster which may never happen is bad enough, but then to suffer a catastrophe and find our insurers quibbling about the claim really makes the blood boil.

Although some insurers are undoubtedly better than others when it comes to dealing with claims, even with the utmost good faith on both sides, things sometimes go wrong, drastically on occasions.

To their credit, insurance companies have recognised that in today's consumer-led society, there is need for procedures to be laid down for their customers, so that the majority of disputes can be investigated and resolved without taking matters to court. These procedures are now set out in policies.

As policyholders, it is necessary for us to be aware of our rights, and the avenues of appeal open to us in the event of a dispute or complaint concerning our claim. If we have a good case we need to be able to use the procedures in a confident and positive manner. After all, they are there for our benefit.

DISPUTING POLICY LIABILITY

These type of disputes go to the root of the insurance contract. In effect, the insurer is stating that your policy does not cover the event or the item for which you are claiming. This can be for a number of reasons, such as:

● disagreement over policy terms
● lack of proof to support claim
● alleged fraud
● non-disclosure of information, material to the insurance
● lack of reasonable care by policyholder
● gross under-insurance.

The dispute or complaint procedures, some of which have been touched on in previous chapters, can vary between different insurers, and according to the type of insurance. But generally, for each type of insurance, the stages are as follows:

Household and motor insurances

1. Speak to the intermediary who sold you the policy, if one is involved.

2. Contact the branch manager or claims manager of the insurance company.

3. Write to the chief general manager of the insurance company at head office (see *The Insurance Directory and Year Book* at your local reference library for the name and address).

4. If you remain dissatisfied, and your insurers are members of the Association of British Insurers, write with full details of the problem to them at 51 Gresham Street, London EC2V 7HQ.

5. If still not satisfied, and your insurer is a member of The Insurance Ombudsman Bureau, you may refer your dispute or complaint to the Bureau.

The above procedures do not affect your legal rights, and do not prevent you from commencing legal proceedings against your insurers.

Business insurances

The same procedures and protections are not available to holders of business policies. As they operate in a commercial world, insurers consider they should have superior knowledge of what they are buying when taking out insurance, and are more likely to have professional advice available.

When a dispute or complaint arises on a claim under your business policy, the options open to you are:

1. Consult the intermediary who sold the policy to you. There is more likely to be a broker or consultant involved in a business policy.

2. Contact the branch manager or claims manager of your insurance company.

3. Write to the chief general manager at the head office of your insurance company.

4. If negotiations with the insurance company fail, appoint a solicitor with a view to taking legal action.

DISPUTING SETTLEMENT AMOUNT

Disputes or complaints in connection with valuation of losses and damage, and the amount of the claim settlement are as common as ever. Three areas where such complaints frequently arise are:

● car insurance
● storm damage
● jewellery claims.

Car insurance

Vehicle valuations continue to cause many problems. In the event of settlement where your car is written-off or stolen, you are entitled to receive the **market value**. This is not the same as the **secondhand value**, which would apply if you were selling the car. The claim must be based on what you have to pay to buy a replacement from a reputable dealer, not a private sale.

Trade guides, such as *Glass's Guide* are helpful, but the real answer is to find a near equivalent vehicle displaying a price on a garage forecourt.

Storm damage

Insurers reduce or even decline claim payments in many cases, due to lack of building maintenance. They argue that, had the property been well-maintained and in sound condition, the damage would not have occurred.

While it has to be accepted that insurance is not a maintenance contract, and cannot pay for previous wear and tear, insurers cannot avoid all responsibility. They have to pay the value of any damage which can be attributed to the storm in question.

Jewellery claims

Jewellery claims remain a constant source of settlement disputes, usually over the valuation issue.

Smaller claims are usually negotiated on the basis of a jeweller's estimate for replacement, prepared from your description after the loss. As long as the claim figure does not seem exaggerated, there is not normally a problem.

Where valuations were supplied at the time the policy was taken out, there can still be difficulties when a claim occurs. Claims are sometimes reduced because the original valuations were too brief or vague, for example, 'gold bangle – £80', 'diamond ring – £400.'

A G Grieved
The Cottage
Tinseltown
TT2 1MC

Mr O Lummy
Manager
Hard Luck Insurance Company
2 Simple Street
Tinseltown TT1 1BC

Address
letter
to
appropriate
person

Dear Mr Lummy
Household contents insurance policy no: 999666
Claim reference: 414243 – Theft 8 December 199X

Give full
policy details
and reference

Thank you for your letter of 15 January 199X
offering £300 for my gold bracelet, stolen when
my cottage was burgled on the 8th December
199X.

Summarise
position
as succinctly
as possible

I took out my policy with your company in March
199X, and at that time, I was asked to provide a
valuation certificate. The bracelet valuation was
£500, which you were happy to accept (a copy of
the valuation is enclosed). The bracelet was
insured on this basis, and I have been paying the
appropriate premiums.

Briefly
describe
problem and
enclose
copies of
relevant
documents

Unless you can give me a satisfactory explanation
for reducing my claim by £200, I shall expect to
receive your amended offer for the amount of £500
within 10 days.

State what
you want, and
set a
deadline

Yours sincerely

Adam Grieved

Encs.

Fig. 15. Specimen letter to insurer disputing settlement offer.

Insurers are in difficulty here, because they readily accepted the valuations at the outset, and to complain about them when a claim arises is unreasonable. Of course, the answer is to obtain proper valuations from the start. Figure 15 is a letter to an insurer disputing a settlement offer for a gold bracelet.

Insurers exercising their option to replace jewellery, rather than making a cash settlement, causes considerable aggravation. If you refuse the replacement jewellery, insurers often offer a reduced cash settlement, after deducting the discount they would have expected to receive from the jeweller supplying the replacements.

In this type of settlement, the deducted discount should be based on fact, and not just a general level of discount insurers would normally expect to receive for such a transaction.

Resolving claim payment disputes

The procedures for resolving disputes over the amount of a claim payment are similar to those available for disputes over policy liability, with one major difference. As the claim has been admitted and the dispute is solely about the amount payable, it will ultimately be referred to **arbitration**, in accordance with the general conditions of the policy.

Going to arbitration

Arbitration is the process by which two parties in dispute agree to appoint a third, but independent person, to resolve their dispute. It is *the only* alternative to going to court, if the parties want a final and legally binding decision. The arbitrator should preferably be an expert in the field of the dispute, unlike a judge in a court, who is only expert in matters of law.

Using the personal insurance arbitration service

In 1981 some insurance companies set up a Personal Insurance Arbitration Service (PIAS), and at present 32 insurance companies participate in the PIAS scheme.

Under the PIAS an independent arbitrator is appointed by the Chartered Institute of Arbitrators, with the insurance company paying the costs of the arbitration.

The normal procedure under the PIAS rules is that both sides submit documentary evidence within set time limits, and the arbitrator then decides the case on this basis. He can request an informal hearing, as can the policyholder, which both parties would have to attend. The arbitrator's decision is final and binding on both you and the insurance company.

The service may be offered by the insurance company to a person insured *under a policy issued in a private capacity*, who claims to have suffered financial loss through the alleged failure of an insurance company to fulfil its obligations under a contract of insurance.

The service is not designed to accommodate disputes in which the issues are complicated, fraud is alleged, or if the matter is likely to require a formal hearing for resolution. Nor does the service apply to:

● disputes involving amounts claimed in excess of £50,000
● insurances effected by employers for the benefit of employees
● policies of industrial life assurance.

Disputes with Lloyd's underwriters

Any policyholder insured through the Lloyd's market who has a dispute cannot contact direct the underwriter who issued his insurance, or the claims manager handling the claim. All complaints have to be channelled through the broker who placed the insurance.

If the broker fails to resolve the problem to your satisfaction, write with full details to the manager of the complaints department at Lloyd's of London.

Lloyd's is a member of The Insurance Ombudsman Bureau, but not the Personal Insurance Arbitration Service.

PURSUING YOUR CASE

When embroiled in a dispute over a claim with your insurer, there is a temptation, perhaps through frustration and anger, to exaggerate your side of the case. Although understandable, your best chance of a successful outcome is to act in good faith.

Keeping clean hands

The certainty is that once your insurers, the IOB or PIAS have reason to doubt you are being fair and honest in your claim, they will decline to help you any further.

This tough attitude has to be viewed against a background of increasing fraud in the insurance industry. According to the Crime and Fraud Prevention Bureau of the ABI, of 5.2 million insurance claims in 1994, as many as 5 per cent were estimated to be fraudulent.

While you may never have intended to be fraudulent in your claim, exaggeration or inaccuracies could easily give rise to suspicion. Having regard to the many recent initiatives adopted by insurers to detect doubtful claims, there is an increasing likelihood of any policyholders attempting to defraud their insurers being found out.

Avoiding delay

Although your complaint should be dealt with on its merits, your case is likely to be weakened by any undue delay on your part. Not only can insurers get annoyed, but more importantly, the longer the time lapse since the events complained of, the less likely you will be able to produce the necessary evidence to win the case on the balance of probabilities. Files may have been closed, leading to a loss of momentum for any relevant investigations required.

Also, unreasonable delay in pursuing a complaint could make it more difficult for the other party to accept your version of events.

Final checking
As a final check when pursuing your disputed claim, ask yourself the following questions:

1. Exactly what am I claiming for?

2. Why do I believe that I am entitled to something?

3. Have I clearly answered all points in the insurer's argument with which I disagree?

4. Have I complied with any relevant time limits?

USING THE INSURANCE OMBUDSMAN

The Insurance Ombudsman Bureau was founded in 1981 by a group of major insurance companies. One of its major functions is to provide an independent and impartial method of resolving certain disputes between insurers and individual policyholders. There are now over 350 members of the Bureau.

There is no charge to the applicant for the ombudsman's services.

What the insurance ombudsman can do for you
He can investigate and decide upon a complaint, dispute or claim between you and your insurer, provided the insurer is a member. The process is speedier than the courts, and the ombudsman deals directly and informally with you.

In relation to a claim, however, the complaint must:

●   first be referred to senior management of your insurer to give them the opportunity to resolve it
●   be passed to the ombudsman within six months of you receiving the final decision from senior management
●   concern you personally (for instance, your car, your household contents)
●   relate to a policy in the UK, Isle of Man or Channel Islands.

Usually, the ombudsman cannot deal with your claim if it is already the subject of legal proceedings or arbitration, the dispute is between you and someone else's insurer, or the policy is a commercial one.

He cannot reopen cases where a decision has previously been made, unless new evidence is available.

How to make a complaint

If your complaint has been considered by your insurer's senior management, and you remain dissatisfied, write to the Insurance Ombudsman Bureau at:

City Gate One
135 Park Street
London SE1 9EA

with an explanation of your dispute. If the ombudsman can take on the matter, he will ask to be provided with all relevant papers.

If you choose to use a solicitor, or other professional, to put your case to the ombudsman, you have to pay the costs involved.

The ombudsman's procedure

On receipt of all the papers, he will study them, and require your insurer to provide all its files on the case. The ombudsman will be assisted by an assistant with legal or insurance qualifications, who may make further enquiries of you. Sometimes, he will refer to experts.

The ombudsman may try to settle the dispute by simply giving advice, or even bringing the two sides together. If this fails, he will make a common sense and fair decision, based on the law and good insurance practice.

The ombudsman's decision

The decision of the ombudsman will be conveyed to you by the Bureau in writing. You can accept or reject the decision.

If the decision is wholly, or partly in your favour, your insurer must pay you any award made up to £100,000.

Should you reject the decision, it is suspended and you are free to do as you wish. A rejected decision does not affect your right to take legal action afterwards.

CHECKLIST

● Follow the complaints/disputes procedures, which are usually set out at the end of most policy booklets.

● If your dispute cannot be settled with your insurance company, check whether your insurer is a member of the Insurance Ombudsman's Bureau or the Personal Insurance Arbitration Service.

● Consider whether you wish to refer your case to the IOB or PIAS, and if so, does it meet the necessary criteria for referral.

● Avoid delay in pursuing your case, and do not exaggerate or make inflated claims.

● Understand how the Insurance Ombudsman's Bureau operates, before applying to the Bureau with your case.

● Rejection of your case by the Ombudsman does not affect your legal rights.

CASE STUDIES

Noah learns his lesson

Noah receives a prompt reply from the head office of his insurers. After investigating his complaint with their local branch and the loss adjuster, they inform Noah that they see no reason to revise the claim settlement proposals.

Noah is furious. He replies to the head office, making the following points:

- he intends to immediately cancel his policies with them
- he will inform his business colleagues and friends of their unreasonable attitude to claims
- he will see his solicitor, with a view to taking legal action against them.

On meeting his solicitor, Perry, Noah pours out his hard-luck story, but finds little sympathy from Perry.

Perry points out to Noah how his approach, both in arranging the insurance and pursuing the claim, has been unfortunate and not helped his cause. He advises Noah to see a broker regarding his future insurance arrangements.

Meanwhile, in connection with the current claim, Perry recommends to Noah that he accepts the settlement on offer, as it appears fair and reasonable. He adds that, if they had wished, insurers could probably have declined liability for the whole claim, due to breaches of several policy conditions.

Noah leaves the solicitor's office, somewhat deflated but wiser.

Dora is let down by her decorators

Dora receives an interim payment cheque for £400 from her insurance company, against her contents claim.

The dry-cleaning bill for £75 arrives and Dora immediately sends it on to her insurers.

Bodgett & Scram the decorators are living up to their name. Not only is the standard of their work poor, but Dora has not seen them for several days. Enquiries reveal they have ceased trading and disappeared from the area.

A worried Dora speaks to her insurers. They suggest she obtains an estimate from another local decorator to complete the contract. The new decorator, Michael Angelo, informs Dora the redecorating will need to be started from scratch again. The cost will be £50 more than Bodgett & Scram's original price. Dora's anxieties increase, particularly as she had paid Bodgett & Scram £30 at the outset to buy materials.

The insurers advise Dora their liability is limited to the original agreed estimate from Bodgett & Scram, as that was the value of the damage. Any extra costs are Dora's concern, as they relate to the breakdown of her contract with the original decorators.

Unhappy, Dora writes to the branch manager of her insurance company, asking to meet him. A meeting is arranged for the following week.

Ella plays for sympathy

Ella completes the prescribed application form for the arbitration procedure, signifying her agreement to be bound by the arbitrator's decisions. Her insurers follow a similar path, so that a joint application is made.

In return, Ella, as claimant, receives notice of acceptance of the application, with a claim form for her to complete.

Shortly afterwards, both parties receive notification of the arbitrator's appointment from the Chartered Institute of Arbitrators.

Ella is given 28 days to complete and submit the completed claim form, with supporting documentation (in duplicate) to the Institute. She is informed that a copy of these claim documents will be forwarded by the Institute to the insurer, who is given 28 days to send a written defence to the claim to the Institute with supporting documents (in duplicate).

A copy of the defence documents will then be sent to Ella, giving her 14 days to comment on them, but she will not be allowed to introduce any new matters. Furthermore, Ella is told that if she fails to meet the required time limits, or give a reasonable explanation for her failure to do so, then she will be treated as having abandoned her claim. If the insurer fails to meet the limits, the arbitration will proceed, based on her claim documents only.

All seems fair to Ella, and she carefully completes her claim form. On preparing her case, Ella pleads ignorance of insurance matters, pressure of business leading to lack of time to study the insurance proposal form, and stresses she simply did what she thought was right after the accident. Having made a mistake when driving her new car, she saw no point in denying it to anyone.

After sending off the documents to the Institute, Ella still hopes her insurers might take a sympathetic view after reading her documents and pay the claim, before the arbitration proceeds.

DISCUSSION POINTS

1. 'Fair and reasonable' is the yardstick adopted by those handling disputes, in trying to reach a just decision. But not everyone will agree on what is fair and reasonable in any particular case.

   As this term cannot be clearly defined, do you agree it should be replaced by some other means of reaching decisions? If so, what means?

2. Insurance policies tend to look at matters as either 'black or white'. Either a claim will succeed, and the policyholder will be paid in full, or the claim will fail and the policyholder will receive nothing.

   Discuss whether you think this approach is fair, having regard to instances where a policyholder *unintentionally* fails to disclose something or misrepresents some issue on the proposal form. Is there a case for a proportional payment?

3. If a policyholder in dispute with his insurer on a claim, takes it to the ombudsman or arbitration, and wins his case, should compensation for inconvenience be awarded over and above the amount payable for the original claim?

10
Concluding Claim Settlement

THINKING POSITIVE

Having suffered the kind of misfortune which means making an insurance claim, the last thing you want when trying to get your property and life back in order, is lengthy and complicated claim negotiations with insurers. Fortunately, most are straightforward, although it is the problem claims that attract publicity.

Whether a claim is straightforward or complicated, one certainty is that a settlement will be reached one day. When that day arrives, you will be keen to tie up any final loose ends as quickly as possible and put the whole unfortunate episode behind you. But, even in these closing stages, there is still need for care and concentration, while maintaining an overall positive attitude. Take time to thoroughly check and understand the forms you will probably be asked to sign by your insurers, loss adjusters or perhaps, tradesmen/suppliers.

SIGNING DISCHARGE FORMS

Some insurance companies, on settlement of a claim, still use **discharge receipts**. Sent with the settlement cheque, these forms are normal receipts quoting your policy number, the date of loss and the sum you have been paid.

There is no problem signing and returning such forms to insurers. See Figure 16 for an example of a discharge form for a motor claim.

Occasionally, forms contain a phrase that the payment is 'in full and final settlement' of your claim. Signing such a discharge apparently precludes you from reopening your claim if further losses or damage should be discovered at a later date. In practice, insurers are usually prepared to reopen claims if genuine additional losses come to light.

Theft claims

On concluding a theft claim, you may need to endorse the discharge receipt or satisfaction note issued by your insurer. With thefts, it can be

143

weeks, or even months, after the break-in before some articles are found to be missing. In such cases, the discharge receipt should be endorsed: 'Based on losses discovered to date. I reserve the right to submit a supplementary claim for any other losses which may later come to light.'

Motor claims

Once repairs to your car have been completed, the repairer will usually expect you to inspect the car. On doing so, ask for a copy of the detailed repair account, describing the work carried out.

You may be asked to sign a collection or satisfaction note stating the repairs have been carried out to your satisfaction. This can then be sent by the garage to your insurer, with their account for payment.

If the repairs are not to your satisfaction, have no qualms about refusing to sign the form.

It may be difficult to judge whether the repairs are satisfactory just by looking at the car. If so, when signing the note, add 'subject to no complaint being raised within 21 days of this date', or whatever seems a reasonable period.

Should you sign the satisfaction note, but the repairs prove unsatisfactory, notify insurers immediately. Ask them to sort the matter out direct with the garage, to ensure the vehicle is properly repaired to your satisfaction.

Loss adjusters

On agreeing claim settlement figures, loss adjusters may ask you to sign one of their acceptance forms. In effect, this states you are prepared to accept the agreed sum in full and final satisfaction of your claim. Often, a declaration is included stating you do not have the same property insured with any other insurer. This is a safeguard against you having dual insurance and claiming the full amount of the same claim from both insurers.

It is doubtful whether these forms are legally binding. Their main function is simply to signify to insurers that the loss adjuster has agreed a settlement figure with you.

If you are unhappy with the form, there is nothing to stop you amending the wording to suit your wishes.

On their theft acceptance forms, loss adjusters sometimes incorporate wording to the effect that if any of the stolen property is traced and later returned to you, you will refund the insurance monies to insurers.

You are not obliged to do this, and you can simply leave the insurance company to dispose of the recovered property as they wish, while you keep the insurance payment. When signing an acceptance form of this type, delete any such clause.

Policyholder's Address:

_____;
_____;
_____;

Date _____;

Dear Sirs,

Claim No_*IK(R)_____;

With reference to the loss of or damage to_____;

registered as_____; on the_____; I/We hereby agree to

accept in full discharge of my/our claim for such loss or damage a cash

payment of _____

_____; (£_____;)

(a) Salvage to become the property of General Accident *

(b) The vehicle being my/our property and is not subject to any Hire Purchase

    Agreement, Leasing Contract or any other financial interest *

(c) The vehicle being subject to a Hire Purchase/Leasing Contract, financial

    agreement with_____;

    _____;*

(d) Registration Document and MOT Certificate enclosed *

    * delete if not applicable

Yours faithfully,

Fig. 16. Specimen discharge form for a motor claim.

145

PAYING THE CLAIM

Once insurers have agreed settlement of your claim, you expect their cheque within a few days. Realistically, payment can take weeks rather than days, particularly if a large sum is involved.

Unless other arrangements have been previously agreed with insurers, the settlement cheque will be sent to you, to pay into your bank account. Once it has been 'cleared' by the bank, which can take up to five working days, you then pay the various suppliers, contractors or others involved in the remedial works.

The process is lengthy and can be frustrating, especially when you have a contractor breathing down your neck for his money. Signing a mandate, authorising direct payment to the contractor, avoids this protracted procedure.

If you are responsible for paying part of a bill, perhaps for a policy excess or betterment, you will have to add your contribution at this stage.

In the case of motor repairs, insurers normally pay the garage/repairer direct.

Acknowledging other interests

Some organisations with a financial stake in the insured property, have their interest noted on the policy. The most common example is the building society, who have an insurable interest as mortgagee. However, it could be a relative as part-owner of a property, or someone from whom you borrowed money to set up your small business.

When a claim is settled, if the other party is named as joint-insured with you on the policy, the settlement cheque will be drawn in both names.

If the other party's interest is simply noted on the policy, the cheque will be drawn in your name, but the other party's agreement will be needed before it is released to you.

Paying third-party claims

Third-party claims against you, either as a householder, motorist or business person, will invariably be handled by your insurers. They will deal direct with the third party or his/her solicitor.

Unless there is a dispute over the question of liability, you may not even be required to give evidence, and the third party's claim may be settled without you being informed of the outcome.

In addition to the amount paid to the third party, settlement by your insurers could include legal costs you incurred with their consent, and any costs awarded by a court.

Of course, if the total exceeds the monetary limit of your policy, you will be left to pay the balance.

Avoiding complications

Complications over insurance payments occasionally arise, adding further stress to what has probably been a painful episode. These are often due to a policyholder's failure to keep the policy up to date.

Examples, where complications arise due to lack of action by a policyholder are:

● Both names of divorced policyholders remain on a policy covering property now in the sole ownership of one of them.

● The death of a policyholder is not notified to insurers.

● A policyholder changes his/her name, possibly after marriage, but this is not recorded on an insurance policy.

● The name of a house or business is altered without insurers being informed.

These snags would be sorted out eventually, but unwanted delays would be inevitable.

RECEIVING *EX GRATIA* PAYMENTS

An *ex gratia* payment by an insurer is one made as a goodwill gesture, but without any legal obligation.

This type of payment is made sparingly, particularly in today's climate of hardening attitudes.

Instances where *ex gratia* payments might be made include:

1. To resolve a dispute where insurers do not wish to alter their stance on policy liability.

2. Where there is serious under-insurance, but no 'average' clause in the policy.

Insurers are entitled to repudiate the claim as you have breached the 'full value warranty' (you agree to insure the property for its full value when taking out the insurance). Although you have no claim, insurers will sometimes offer you an *ex gratia* payment (calculated as if 'average' had been applied to the claim), provided you agree to an immediate increase of the sum insured to the proper level.

Because *ex gratia* payments are no more than favours, made without admission of liability, the following points apply:

● If you think the *ex gratia* payment offered is too low, you have no right to demand an increase – in fact, the original offer may be withdrawn.

● *Ex gratia* payments cannot be included in any subsequent legal action, as they are made outside the policy.

KNOWING YOUR POSITION ON TAX AND DUTY

In relation to household, motor and small business claims, payments received from insurers in settlement of claims are not normally taxable. The payments are not income, but compensation for losses or damage.

However, a consequential loss claim payment under a business policy, put simply, replaces the gross profit lost as a result of the insured damage. So the payment will go through the business's accounts with the other profit for that year, and be **subject to tax** in the usual way.

Paying VAT

Unless you are VAT registered, claim payments by insurers have to include the VAT element within the price of the replacement or repair. Insurers are unable to recover this tax through their own VAT account.

In the case of a business registered as taxable for VAT purposes, as the business can recover the VAT on purchases by offsetting it against VAT charged on sales, no VAT will be included in any claim payment by insurers.

Paying customs duty

If you buy an article abroad, particularly jewellery, gold, or some other precious item, it should be declared on re-entering this country, and a customs declaration obtained. Failure to produce such a declaration may result in insurers trying to decline liability, if the item should later be the subject of a claim.

Motor accidents abroad

You may become liable for foreign customs duty on your car if you take it abroad and cannot bring it back to the UK, either because it is a total loss after an accident, or is stolen. Provision of customs indemnity is a contingency normally covered by your motor policy, but always check before travelling.

RECOVERING MONEY FROM A THIRD PARTY

The term **subrogation** is encountered from time to time. Should the loss or damage for which you pursue a claim under your own policy be the fault of some other person, your insurers have the right to take legal action *in your name* against that person, to recover their outlay. Insurers are said to **exercise their right to subrogation**.

Although the legal action will be in your name, insurers pay the costs involved, as the action is for their benefit. But if you have any uninsured losses insurers may agree to try to recover these at the same time. They may ask you to contribute to the legal or other costs involved.

It is a policy condition that you must give insurers all the assistance they may need to pursue the case against the other party.

DEALING WITH SALVAGE

A general condition of policies is that after a loss, your insurers may enter any building where loss or damage has occurred, and deal with any salvage in a reasonable manner. But you cannot simply abandon any damaged property to them. You are under a duty to salvage what you can, and keep it safe.

When submitting your claim, on the claim form you are asked to estimate the value of any remains of a damaged article. Once insurers have paid you for a replacement, the salvage of the damaged item becomes their property.

You can offer to buy the salvage, but alternatively, insurers may seek to sell it elsewhere, perhaps by obtaining competitive tenders from dealers.

A similar situation exists where your car claim is settled on a total loss basis by insurers. They retain the salvage of the damaged vehicle.

CHECKLIST

● Be cautious when signing discharge receipts or similar forms, and delete or amend those sections with which you disagree.

● In most cases, the settlement cheque will be sent to you, leaving you to pay contractors, suppliers or others involved with repairs or replacements.

● In the case of motor claims involving repairs to your car, insurers normally pay the garage/repairer direct.

● By signing a written mandate, you can authorise your insurer to send a settlement cheque to another party.

- If your policy is in joint names, all cheques issued by insurers will be drawn in those joint names.

- Insurers must acknowledge the interest of any other party noted on the policy when issuing settlement cheques, such as a mortgagee.

- Third-party claims against you by some other person will be handled throughout by your insurers, and they will pay the third party direct in most cases.

- Keep your policy up to date, notifying any alternation in your domestic circumstances, such as divorce or change of address.

- *Ex gratia* payments are sometimes made by insurers 'as a favour', where there is no liability under a policy.

- Insurance claim settlements are not generally taxable, with the notable exception of loss of profits payments.

- Unless you are VAT registered as 'taxable', insurers will include the VAT element in any claim payment.

- If you buy an article abroad, particularly a valuable, obtain a customs declaration on re-entering this country.

- Once insurers have settled your claim, they can exercise their right to subrogation, to recover their outlay from the party legally responsible for the damage, in your name but at their expense.

CASE STUDIES

Noah has one final shot at increasing his settlement offer

Noah, after meeting his solicitor, reflects on his actions throughout the claim. He knows his attitude has been negative and careless. Although realising there is little chance of success, Noah cannot resist one more attempt at obtaining an increased settlement offer.

He telephones Ivor to query the valuation placed on his office contents of £3,000 in the 'average' calculation, which reduced the amount payable from £900 to £600. Ivor is able to prove to Noah that, in fact, the value is slightly more than £3,000.

'How about an *ex gratia* payment?' asks Noah, tongue in cheek.

Ivor says he will speak to insurers, but feels there is no justification for a goodwill gesture in this case.

The next day Ivor confirms there will be no *ex gratia* payment offered, and the original settlement figure stands. Reluctantly, Noah accepts. Ivor sends Noah an acceptance form for the agreed settlement, which he signs and sends back by return.

Noah chases Ivor for the settlement cheque almost daily. It arrives after ten days, to end an unsatisfactory insurance claim.

Dora concludes her claim settlement satisfactorily

Dora receives a further cheque for £75 from her insurers, for the dry-cleaning charge. That settles her contents claim at a total of £475.

As regards C. A. Chance's claim against her for smoke damage to his decorations, Dora learns from another neighbour that Mr Chance has received a cheque for £50 from her insurers, against his claim of £200.

The following week Dora attends the arranged meeting with Mr Goodman, the branch manager of her insurance company.

She informs him of the problems concerning the redecoration, due to Bodgett & Scram's poor work and failure to complete the job.

Mr Goodman is sympathetic, and while he maintains the information given to Dora by his staff was correct, he appreciates the problem is not of her making.

In the circumstances, he agrees that insurers will pay a revised buildings claim, based on the fresh estimate from Michael Angelo. As for the £30 already paid to Bodgett & Scram by Dora, Mr Goodman says he does not believe insurers are liable. Strictly speaking, she should pursue action to recover that sum from Bodgett & Scram, in view of their poor work. However, he appreciates this is not possible and therefore, he will authorise an *ex gratia* payment of 50 per cent, that is £15. Dora accepts this offer.

Michael Angelo completes the work, and his bill is sent to insurers. Dora receives the insurer's cheque a week later, with a discharge receipt, which she promptly signs and returns.

Michael Angelo is paid and with the whole issue closed, Dora is able to get on with the rest of her life.

Ella is involved in another accident!

Ella receives a copy of her insurer's defence for the arbitration. She realises her position is very weak.

The arbitrator's decision comes as no surprise. As he had not found any failure by the insurance company to fulfil its obligation under the contract of insurance, there is no award to her.

Ella soon has another accident in her car, crashing into someone's garden wall, but with no other vehicle involved.

This time, she passes details of her insurance, with her name and address to the owner of the wall, Mr Walldown, but does not admit liability.

Although her off-side front wing and a headlight are damaged, Ella is able to drive the car away from the scene.

Ella immediately reports the accident to her insurance company and brokers. She completes an accident report form.

At her insurer's request, Ella takes her car to a garage near her home, which operates their recommended repair scheme. The garage is able to start the repairs immediately, with insurer's approval. Ella is informed by the garage she will have to pay her £100 excess to them on completion.

Within three days, Ella's car is ready for collection. She inspects her car to ensure the repair is satisfactory, pays her excess, signs a satisfaction note and drives away.

The next week, a builder's estimate for £300 arrives from Mr Walldown for repairs to his wall. Ella passes it to her insurers, commenting that she thinks it is excessive.

DISCUSSION POINTS

1. Insurers increasingly offer discounted cash settlements for claims involving valuables. Settlement is based on the value of the item, less the discount insurers say they can obtain for supplying a replacement item.

    Discuss the fairness of this arrangement.

2. An insurer accepts a claim for damage to a policyholder's car, but insists on a particular garage carrying out the repairs, on the policyholder instruction.

    The repairs prove to be defective, necessitating the work being carried out again elsewhere.

    Who should pay the extra cost of the second repair, and why?

3. According to ABI statistics, the total bill for fraudulent insurance claims in 1994 was £600 million. On average, this costs each of us £10 every time we renew our policies.

    What measures do you suggest insurers can take in arranging settlement of claims to combat this alarming situation?

11
Insuring for the Future

THINKING POSITIVE

Insurance should be looked upon as an investment, but not in the normal sense, where you expect to get back more than you put in. You only see a return on your insurance premiums if you suffer a loss.

The investment is one of time and care, so that when arranging future protection of your assets, you are able to look beyond the marketing blurb and jargon surrounding so many policies, to enable you to arrange a suitable portfolio of insurance covers at the right price for you. Unfortunately, it is often the case that only after suffering a loss do we take a positive attitude towards insurance for the future.

If we are ever to get away from viewing insurance as no more than 'a necessary evil', then the insurance industry needs to concentrate more effort on educating the public, and less on fuelling cut-throat competition, with short-term special offers and added fringe benefits. After all, both insurers and insureds want the same thing in the end, *value for money*.

PENALISING CLAIMS

Household insurances

Many people believe that after a claim, particularly a sizeable one, their premium for the following year will automatically be increased. This is not the case. A claim should have no bearing on the next premium, unless there is a 'no claim discount' applicable.

However, insurance companies will penalise policyholders who are considered to be poor risks, possibly because they:

● are claims conscious (too many claims)

● are suspected of submitting a fraudulent claim

● failed to implement insurers' requirements to safeguard insured property

● consistently show lack of reasonable care

● are troublesome, constantly harassing insurance company staff

● delay having remedial works carried out, so increasing the risk of similar damage recurring.

The type of penalties exercised by insurers can include:

● refusal to renew the policy at next renewal date
● increase in premium
● increase of policy excesses
● where remedial work is delayed, the policy may be renewed but cover excluded for that property still to be repaired, or the peril concerned (for example, subsidence or flood).

Motor insurances

Motor claims are different from other claims, primarily because there is a no-claim discount (NCD) affected, or if there is a protected NCD, a layer of that protection will be stripped off.

If you have an accident and claim, irrespective of whether you were at fault, your discount will be reduced by insurers at next renewal, increasing your premium payment. This applies even if your car is damaged by some unknown driver in a car park, and you were blameless.

Should your insurers be able to recover the cost of the claim from the party responsible your no claims discount need not be affected.

Where you have a bad accident record, or have been convicted of motoring offences, your insurers may penalise you, usually in one of two ways:

● either by increasing your premium, or
● refusing to offer you renewal terms for the next year.

Small business insurances

As with household insurances, insurers do not automatically increase your premium because of a claim.

For a small business run from home, the attitude of insurers towards future insurance cover is much the same as for household insurance, except they may be more demanding when it comes to improvements to minimise the chances of a future recurrence of the loss.

Such demands are often made after theft claims. Insurers may require additional security measures, such as:

- installation of an intruder alarm system, as approved or suggested by them
- security grills, or bars fitted to windows
- security locks and/or bolts fitted to doors/windows
- installation of a safe, to an approved specification
- tightening of system used for banking cash.

These measures will be at your expense, and if not carried out, insurers may decline to renew the policy.

CHANGING INSURANCE COMPANIES

Most insurance policies are annual contracts, so each year you have the opportunity to change insurance companies. This happens to an increasing degree, especially where motor policies are concerned, due to rapidly fluctuating premium rates.

Shopping around each year, or using a broker/consultant to do it for us, is the only means of finding the perfect formula of the right price, combined with effective protection.

As buyers of insurance, we are in a stronger position than we have been for many years. So many insurers are competing for the available business, which has tended to drive prices down. Our newspapers, magazines and televisions are daily carriers of advertisements for cheaper household and motor insurances.

Being aware of the dangers

While it may be prudent to change insurance companies to obtain the best deal available, there are some dangers.

1. If a claim is still outstanding with the original insurer, it should still be dealt with in a fair and reasonable way. But inevitably, there is no longer a goodwill factor, should a dispute arise.

2. Anyone who regularly changes insurance companies can arouse a little suspicion in the insurance market, especially if there have been a number of claims.

3. Should you decide to change insurance companies because you are unwilling to comply with an insurance company's recommendations (such as better security precautions), you may be in difficulty when completing the new proposal form. You will have to answer 'yes' to the question: 'Have you had any insurance or proposal cancelled, withdrawn, declined or made the subject of special terms?' The new

insurer will want to know the terms you refused, and will almost certainly demand the same.

VALUING YOUR PROPERTY AFTER A LOSS

One question which causes confusion among policyholders is what happens to the sum insured after a loss? If you have suffered a burglary for example, you no longer have that stolen property, until such time as it is replaced.

This is just one of several questions frequently asked after a loss has occurred. The following illustrations may help to clarify certain aspects.

Household (post-loss valuation)

Most policies include an **automatic reinstatement clause**, to ensure the sum insured is not exhausted or reduced after a claim. This is usually subject to you implementing any recommendations by insurers to prevent further damage, and there being no delay on your part in having the damage made good.

Check this clause is present in your policy. If not, contact your insurers, broker or agent and request that the sum insured is reinstated to its original level when the loss/damage has been put right.

Strictly speaking, a further premium should be paid for the reinstated amount, calculated pro rata from the date the damage was put right to renewal date. Usually, insurers will not bother, particularly if the sum is small.

In the case of a theft, after the claim has been paid, any specified items which were stolen are automatically deleted from the policy, until such time as you buy replacements. Then, you will need to give necessary details of the replacements to insurers, so that sums insured can be reinstated.

Although not related to a loss situation, if you buy something new for the home, perhaps a three-piece suite, and wish to increase your sum insured for household contents, insurers will often increase the cover immediately, but not charge any increased premium until next renewal date.

Motor (post-loss valuation)

The estimated value inserted in a policy for a car is intended to represent its current market value. If valued too highly your premium will be affected. If too low, any total loss settlement will be unsatisfactory, as payment will be based on market value at the time of loss, or the estimated value in the policy, whichever is the lower. Do not be too modest in your valuation.

In the event of a claim involving repairs to your car, insurers will not be liable for any reduction in the market value following these repairs. This will affect any future 'total loss' payment. Otherwise, apart from loss of no-claims discount, the policy is unaffected.

Should your car be destroyed or stolen, and you have to buy a new one, a fresh insurance contract will be arranged on revised terms, with a recalculated premium.

If you change your car in the normal course of events, unconnected with a claim, you must give insurers full details of the new car without delay. Your existing certificate of insurance may not specify the previous car's registration number, in which case insurers will not issue a new certificate. There may be extra premium to pay for the interim period till next renewal, or even a refund of premium.

Business (post-loss valuation)

Business policies are usually annual contracts, where you pay a premium each year for a specified amount of insurance cover. The onus is on you, as policyholder, to nominate the sums to be insured for each policy section.

With commercial insurance, the sum insured is reduced by the amount of any loss for which a payment is made by insurers. To reinstate the sum insured to the original level, you have to pay an extra premium for the current year, for the period from when the loss was made good, up until next renewal. Generally, there is not an 'automatic reinstatement clause', as found in household policies.

ADAPTING TO A CHANGING MARKET

In this era of wholesale computerisation and widespread downsizing, the insurance industry is being forced to adapt. Not only is the technological revolution having to be faced, but also fierce overseas competition.

This has meant the qualities and skills demanded of staff are changing. **Improved productivity** is the key phrase, with insurance companies using new techniques, such as data processing and electronic document management.

But as customers, how do we fit in to this changing scene?

Insurers are conscious of the need to improve customer satisfaction. This is particularly important in the field of claims, the sharp end of the market, where an advantage can be gained over competitors.

Even so, the evidence suggests there remains a wide chasm between our expectations, as customers, and the product delivered by insurers.

Sources of dissatisfaction

The main sources of dissatisfaction would seem to be:

- lack of personal touch, as local insurance company branch offices have closed

- lack of sensitivity by claims staff

- the cost of some insurance, particularly motor

- failure by insurers to spell out the information they require at proposal form stage, leading to problems over non-disclosure and/or misrepresentation

- the loading of premiums according to your postcode

- while most insurance policies are now in plain English style, the vocabulary of the contract in some policies still baffles consumers, and there is too much small print

- delay in processing claims, especially if the claim does not fit neatly in to one of the usual pigeon-holes, or if the loss is covered by more than one policy.

What about the policyholder?

In this rapidly changing world, insurance continues to grow in importance but at the same time, it becomes more complex and confusing for the policyholder.

Just as insurers have been forced to alter their systems and attitudes, so must we, the policyholders.

Long-term loyalty is a thing of the past, and is rarely rewarded by insurers. As policyholders, we must be businesslike, and constantly look for the best deal for us. If that means leaving an insurer with whom we have been insured for many years, so be it.

We must also lose our customary British reticence to question things we do not understand. When a claim arises, and there is something wrong, the only one to suffer will be you.

- If you do not understand some clause in a proposal form, policy or claim form – **seek clarification.**

- If you do not agree with any aspect of a claim – **say so and confirm in writing.**

- If you are not happy with the person dealing with your case – **ask for someone else to be appointed.**

● If you do not like your current insurers for whatever reasons – **look to change at the earliest opportunity**.

The message behind these examples is that, as customers, **we have the power to get the sort of insurance market we want**.

CHECKLIST

● In household insurances, next year's premium is not normally increased because you have made a claim.

● Householders may be penalised by insurers if they are considered poor risks (for example, suspected of fraud or 'claim happy').

● A motor insurance claim affects your next year's premium because you lose some of your no claims discount.

● Motor insurers may increase your premium, or even refuse to offer renewal terms if you have a bad accident record, or if you are convicted of motoring offences.

● After a business claim, there is no automatic increase in your next premium, but insurers often insist on improvements being carried out at the risk address, to minimise the chances of a future recurrence.

● When changing to another insurance company, be aware of the possible dangers if you still have a claim outstanding, change too frequently, or if you are changing to avoid complying with your current insurers's recommendations.

● Most household policies include an automatic reinstatement clause, so that your sum insured is automatically restored to its original level after a claim.

● In motor insurance, if you claim on your policy for a repair, in most cases it will not affect the estimated value of the vehicle shown on the certificate of insurance.

● If the car is stolen or destroyed, a new insurance contract on fresh terms will have to be arranged for any replacement vehicle.

● After a loss, the sum insured on a business policy is reduced by that amount (you will have to pay extra premium for the remainder of the current year to reinstate the sum insured).

● As policyholders we have to adapt and alter our previous attitude towards insurance, if we are to get the type of insurance market we want.

CASE STUDIES

Noah gets experts advice on his insurance

Noah explores the possibility of changing his insurers, but finds matters more complex than expected. On the advice of his long-suffering secretary, Anita, he approaches a local registered insurance broker.

On talking to the broker, Noah finally realises he knows far less about the insurance world than he thought. Under the broker's guidance, Noah's insurances are reorganised and set up in a proper manner to give his business all the necessary covers at a reasonable price. Noah is able to concentrate on the business he knows best, surveying.

Dora has become a strong supporter of insurance

Dora remains with her original insurers, and due to her claim, fully appreciates the benefit of insurance. She makes sure her friends and relatives are also well informed on the subject.

Dora diligently reviews her policies each renewal, making enquiries to ensure her insurance arrangements remain suitable and cost-effective, for her particular needs.

Ella has learnt from her mistakes

Ella is a changed person regarding the subject of insurance. Hers has proved a very costly learning process, but nowadays, she reads her motor policy from start to finish at each renewal. Every doubtful point is queried, and she does everything 'by the book'.

Ella's premiums remain high, but she is determined to restore her no-claims discount to the maximum 60 per cent as soon as possible. Despite her recent bad claims experience, insurers have continued to offer renewal terms.

DISCUSSION POINTS

1. What steps do you think the insurance industry could take to improve its public image?

2. The British insurance market is generally considered to be the best in

the world. That being so, why do you think so many of our insurance companies are being threatened, or even taken over, by foreign competitors?

3.   'I'm not worried how much it costs, my insurance company will deal with it', or 'I always add about 20 per cent to my claim, after all, insurance companies can afford it'. Do you think these commonly heard statements are simply irresponsible, or should they be regarded as conspiracy to commit fraud?

Glossary

Accident report form. The form your insurers require you to complete after any accident or incident involving your car, even if you do not intend to claim on your policy.

Agent. A person who introduces business to an insurer for commission, but can act for either insurers or insured.

All-risk. Insurance which covers every happening, except those specifically excluded in the policy.

Arbitration. Settlement of a dispute by an independent person, whose decision is to be accepted by both parties. It is an alternative to legal action.

Average. A policy condition where if you are under-insured, you have to pay a rateable proportion of any loss. Insurer's payment is calculated in the same proportion as the sum insured bears to the actual value of the property insured.

Betterment. Measure of benefit to the policyholder, as a result of the works carried out to achieve claim settlement. This amount is payable by the policyholder.

Broker. An intermediary registered with the Insurance Broker's Registration Council. A broker acts as an agent for insurers, and on behalf of the insured.

Certificate of motor insurance. A standard document issued by insurers to confirm insurance cover meeting the requirements of the Road Traffic Acts has been taken out.

Comprehensive. Insurance which provides cover against specified perils listed in the policy. (It does not cover all forms of loss or damage, as some people mistakenly believe.)

Conditions (policy). Stipulations written in a policy, with which a policyholder must comply. Failure to do so many result in insurers refusing to pay a claim.

Contribution. When more than one policy covers the same risk, each insurer contributes by paying its rateable proportion of any loss.

Cover note. Particularly in motor insurance, a document issued by insurers confirming temporary insurance cover, until the proper certificate of insurance is issued.

Days of grace. Number of days for which insurance cover continues beyond the actual expiry date of a policy, that you intend to renew. If you fail to pay the renewal premium within this period, your policy lapses. Motor policies have no days of grace.

Declaration. Insured's signed statement at the foot of a proposal or claim form, certifying the information given is accurate.

Duty of disclosure. Obligation placed on someone taking out insurance, to inform insurers of anything that could influence their judgement on whether the risk is acceptable, or the terms to be offered. The obligation exists even if there is no specific question asked on the matter in the proposal form.

Endorsement. An amendment or alteration to a policy, which becomes an integral part of that policy.

Excess (or deductible). Specified initial amount of a claim which the insured has to bear. If a claim fails to exceed this amount stated in the policy, no payment is due from insurers.

Exclusion or exception. An event specifically excluded from the terms of a policy.

Ex gratia. Payment made 'as a favour' by an insurer, when there is no obligation under the policy terms.

Extension. An addition to an existing policy, perhaps to cover an extra item or an added risk. An alternative to issuing a fresh policy.

Green card. Internationally recognised document that can be issued to motorists travelling abroad, to show their UK motor insurance has been extended in full to cover driving in specified foreign countries.

Indemnity. Insurance principle by which a policyholder is placed in the same financial position after a loss, as he was immediately before it.

Index-linking. System for automatically increasing a sum insured in line with official price increase statistics.

Insurable interest. The extent to which a person would suffer a financial loss if certain property or goods were damaged, destroyed or lost.

Knock-for-knock. Agreement in motor insurance when each insurer pays for damage to its own policyholder's car, irrespective of who was to blame.

Liability. Legal responsibility for injury to other persons or damage to their property.

Limit of indemnity. Maximum sum an insurer can be expected to pay under a policy, or section of a policy.

Loss adjuster. Independent professional claims expert (excluding motor), who is engaged by insurers to impartially check and arrange settlement of claims in accordance with policy terms.

Loss assessor. Person specialising in compiling and negotiating settlement of claims on behalf of policyholders, by whom he is paid.

Material fact. Any fact which could influence an underwriter in his acceptance of the risk, or fixing the premium rate.

New-for-old. Insurance where a claim is settled on the basis of destroyed/lost property being replaced by new.

No-claim discount (NCD). Mostly used in motor insurance, a percentage deduction from a premium at renewal where there has been no claim in the previous year(s).

Ombudsman. Official, financed by participating insurers, to whom unresolved complaints can be referred.

Peril. Event which may be covered by or excluded from an insurance policy.

Peril (special). Term used by insurers for insured events added to a policy not originally designed to cover those events (for example, burst pipes and storm perils added to a fire policy).

Proposal form. Document completed by prospective policyholder, giving details required by insurers to enable them to decide whether to accept the risk and at what premium. Once agreed by both parties, it forms the basis of the insurance contract.

Proximate cause. The root or initial cause in a chain of event, which is the one responsible for the loss or damage (for example, extinguishment water damage has a proximate cause of fire).

Pro-rata premium. Charge for a number of days a risk is covered, calculated as a precise fraction of the annual premium.

Reinstatement. When insurers elect to replace or repair damaged property rather than pay a cash settlement. Or restoration of the sum insured to the original level after a loss.

Renewal. Continuation of a policy for a further term, on payment of a fresh premium.

Replacement-as-new. Insurance where claims are dealt with on the basis of the cost of a new equivalent to the lost or destroyed item, without deduction for age, wear and tear.

Risk. The property insured, as opposed to the perils which may damage that property, (for example, the risk could be a small detached cottage).

Schedule. Policy section setting out the main details of the insured, property to be covered, the period of cover, and the application of any special terms, plus other details specific to the particular insurance and premium.

Subrogation. Insurer's right to pursue action in the policyholder's name against the party considered legally liable to the policyholder for the loss or damage.

Sum insured. The amount of cover set against each item in an insurance policy, representing insurer's maximum liability for the particular item.

Third party. Person who is injured or whose property is damaged by the policyholder (the first party) – the second party is the insurer.

Total loss. The total destruction of something; when the cost of repairing a damaged item is more than its pre-damage value (constructive total loss); and when a sum insured is paid in full.

Utmost good faith. Duty placed on both parties to insurance contract. The insured has to disclose all facts material to the risk while insurers have to treat the policyholder fairly.

Warranty. A condition which goes to the root of a policy and must be strictly complied with for a claim to be paid under the policy (for example, an intruder alarm system must be regularly maintained in full working order).

Useful Addresses

Association of British Insurers (ABI), 51 Gresham Street, London EC2V 7HQ. Tel: (0171) 600 3333.

The Chartered Institute of Arbitrators/Personal Insurance Arbitration Service (PIAS), International Arbitration Centre, 24 Angel Gate, City Road, London EC1V 2RS. Tel: (0171) 837 4483.

British Insurance and Investment Brokers' Association (BIIBA), BIIBA House, 14 Bevis Marks, London EC3A 7NT. Tel: (0171) 623 9043.

The Insurance Ombudsman Bureau, City Gate One, 135 Park Street, London SE1 9EA. Tel: (0171) 928 7600.

Subsidence Claims Advisory Bureau, Charter House, 43 St Leonard's Road, Bexhill-on-Sea, East Sussex TN40 1JA. Tel: (01424) 733727.

The Chartered Institute of Loss Adjusters, Manfield House, 1 Southampton Street, London WC2R 0LR. Tel: (0171) 240 1496.

Institute of Public Loss Assessors, 14 Red Lion Street, Chesham, Bucks HP5 1HB. Tel: (01494) 782342.

Institute of Automotive Engineer Assessors, Mansell House, 22 Bore Street, Lichfield, Staffs WS13 6LP. Tel: (01543) 251346.

Insurance Brokers Registration Council, 15 St Helen's Place, London EC3A 6DS. Tel: (0171) 588 4387.

The Chartered Insurance Institute, 31 Hillcrest Road, South Woodford, London E18 2JP. Tel: (0181) 989 8464.

Motor Insurers' Bureau, 152 Silbury Boulevard, Central Milton Keynes, Bucks MK9 1NB. Tel: (01908) 240000.

Lloyd's, 1 Lime Street, London EC3M 7HA. Tel: (0171) 327 5658.

Further Reading

A Guide to the UK Insurance Industry, Price Waterhouse (Graham & Trotman, 1990).

Company Insurance Handbook, edited by Association of Insurance and Risk Managers in Industry and Commerce (Gower, 1984).

Dictionary of Insurance Law, E. R. Hardy Ivamy (Butterworths, 1981).

Essential Cases in Insurance Law, Kenneth Cannar (Woodhead-Faulkner, Ltd, 1985).

Fire and Motor Insurance, E. R. Hardy Ivamy (Butterworths, 1984).

How To Start a Business From Home, Graham Jones (How To Books, 1994).

How To Work From Home, Ian Phillipson (How To Books, 1995).

Modern Insurance Law, John Bird (Sweet & Maxwell, 1988).

Tolley's Insurance Handbook, Robert M. Merkin (Tolleys, 1994).

United Kingdom Glossary of Insurance Terms, (Ernst & Young, 1995).

Witherby's Dictionary of Insurance, Hugh Cockerell (Witherby's 1980).

Index

acceptance forms, 144
accessories (car), 35
aerials, 33
agents, 57, 59, 64
all risks, 39, 124
alternative accommodation, 18, 92, 118, 120
'any-driver' policies, 21
arbitration, 136
Association of British Insurers, 41, 70, 109, 133
automatic reinstatement clause, 156
'average' clause, 117, 122, 124, 147

Banks, 57, 59, 112
betterment, 121
block policies, 12
book value, 121
borrowed vehicle, 21
British Insurance and Investment Brokers' Association, 58
brokers, 50, 57, 58, 64, 71, 75
buildings (definition), 12, 13
Building societies, 11, 57, 59, 61, 93, 112

claim form, 73, 90, 99
claims inspector, 73
comprehensive cover, 19, 35, 122
computers, 36, 50
consequential loss, 26, 37, 50, 124
consultant, 57, 59, 64, 71, 75
contents (definition), 14
contract of insurance, 57, 62
cookers, 15
court awards, 18
credit cards, 18
customs duty, 148

dangerous premises, 37
days of grace, 66

death benefit, 18, 35
declaration, 62
demolition costs, 45
discharge receipts, 143
domestic staff, 14, 25
dual insurance, 17, 27

earthquakes, 32, 33
employees' effects, 36
employer's liability, 26, 36
ex gratia payments, 147
explosion, 32

fatal accident provision, 121
fidelity insurance, 41
finance companies, 92, 93
flood, 33
fraud, 126, 132, 153
freezer contents, 14, 19
full value warranty, 147

glass breakage, 16, 40
Glass's Guide, 81
good faith, 61, 81, 137
goods in transit, 41
guest's property, 25

helplines, 72, 83
high risk items, 14, 120

impact, 33
indemnity cover, 45, 80, 91, 116, 120, 122
indemnity period, 124
index-linking, 41, 45
instalment schemes, 63
Institute of Automotive Engineer Assessors, 125
Institute of Public Loss Assessors, 85
insurable interest, 146
Insurance Brokers Registration Council, 58

Insurance Ombudsman Bureau 108, 133, 137, 138
interim payments (payments on account), 127
interior decorations, 15

knock-for-knock, 122

leased equipment, 93
legal expenses, 40, 146
legal liability, 18, 25, 34, 98, 121
letting property, 24, 25
lightning, 32
limited new-for-old, 49, 120
limits of indemnity, 50
Lloyd's, 58, 137
locks and keys clause, 18, 120
loss adjusters, 73, 83, 144
loss assessors, 74, 85
loss notification, 71

malicious damage, 25, 33
mandate, 127
market value, 118, 121, 134, 156
matching items clause, 118, 120
material fact, 61, 132
medical expenses, 21, 35
money, 26, 28, 29, 121
motor accident report form, 91
motor engineers, 74

named driver policies, 21
negligence, 36, 37–38
new-for-old, 49, 80, 91
no-claims discounts, 16, 53, 121, 153, 154
non-disclosure, 132

office equipment, 36
oil leakage, 16, 34
own labour, 81

passengers (car), 21
personal accident cover, 19
personal effects, 14, 21, 36, 39, 101
Personal Insurance Arbitration Service, 136, 137
pollution, 37
premium payment, 51, 58, 63, 66
product liability, 26, 38
professional fees, 17, 45
professional indemnity, 38
proposal forms, 57, 61, 155

protected no-claims discounts, 122, 154
public liability, 25, 26, 37

reasonable care, 132, 154
reinstatement, 82, 157
renewal, 65
rent, 17, 118, 120
replacement-as-new, 19, 45, 49, 118, 122
replacement option, 126, 136
riot, 33
Road Traffic Acts, 19, 38

salvage, 72, 149
sanitary fixtures, 16, 17
satellite aerials, 15, 19, 33
satisfaction notes, 143, 144
schedule, 65, 71
smoke damage, 32, 33
sports equipment, 14, 19
stock, 36, 50
storm, 33
subrogation, 148
subsidence, 32, 124
supplementary claims, 97, 99

tax, 25, 148
tenant's liability, 18
theft, 16, 25, 33, 128, 143
third-party damage/injury, 18
third party, fire and theft, 19, 35
third party only cover, 19, 34
tied agents, 64
total loss, 112, 113, 121, 156
trees, 34

underground pipes/cables, 17
under-insurance, 122, 132
unoccupancy, 15, 16, 34, 53

valuables, 39
valuation (cars), 24, 156
valuation (property), 45, 100, 134, 156
value added tax, 148
valued policies, 125
vandalism, 98
vicarious liability, 37

water damage, 34
wear and tear, 35, 91, 118
windscreens, 21, 36, 112

COLLECTING A DEBT
How to enforce payment of money owed to you

Roy Hedges

Effective use of the County and Small Claims Courts will make your delinquent customers cough-up, providing your business with positive cash flow. It will also stop your wayward customers using your business as a source of interest free credit. Without using a solicitor, it will be possible for you to collect money owed, claim interest on outstanding debts, and settle long-standing warranty disputes with shops or manufacturers. It matters not if you are a single trader, a small business or a large organisation. This guide on how the County and Small Claims Courts operate will save you time, money and frustration, demonstrating ruses the legal profession use, such as why it is better to get judgement in the Lower Courts and transfer your case to a Higher Court for enforcement. Roy Hedges has spent many years working as a Collection manager for a leading trade finance company and as Director of their leasing subsidiary. He frequently addresses manufacturing and trade associations gatherings on credit control, customer service, cash collection and related subjects. He lives in Romford, Essex.

160pp. illus. 1 85703 131 8.

PREPARING A BUSINESS PLAN
How to lay the right foundations for business success

Matthew Record

A business plan is the most important commercial document you will ever have to produce, whether you are just starting out in business, or are already trading. A well thought out and carefully structured plan will be crucial to the survival and longterm success of the enterprise. It will provide a detailed map of exactly where it is going, and help you forestall any problems long before they arise. A third of all new businesses fail in their first year, and of the rest a staggering 95 per cent will not make it beyond 5 years. Poor planning has been identified as the major cause of business failure. With the odds so stacked against success, make sure YOUR business gets off to the right start. Matthew Record is a business consultant specialising in the preparation of business plans for a variety of commercial clients. His company, Phoenix Business Plans, is based in Dorset.

158pp illus. 1 85703 374 4. 2nd edition.

INVESTING IN STOCKS AND SHARES
A step-by-step handbook for the prudent investor

Dr John White

This book has been specially updated to help and guide those with a lump sum or surplus income to invest and who are considering investing all or part of this sum in quoted securities. Dr John White, an Oxford graduate, is himself an experienced investor and adviser to an investment company. He has a professional background in computers and has produced a range of software for chart analysis. 'User-friendly . . . Contains many practical examples and illustrations of typical share-dealing documents. There are also case studies which give you a feel for your own inclinations about risk versus profit . . . Demystifies the world of stocks and shares.' *OwnBase*. 'Will be a help to private investors . . . Gives an easy to understand guide to the way the stockmarket works, and how the investor should go about setting up a suitable investment strategy.' *What Investment*.

224pp illus. 1 85703 369 8. 3rd edition.

COPING WITH SELF ASSESSMENT
How to complete your tax return and minimise your tax bill

John Whiteley

The Inland Revenue is sending out a colossal nine million tax returns in 1997 for the new self assessment system. The new forms and the new system of self assessing and paying tax represent a radical departure from the previous way of doing things. This book explains step-by-step how the new system works, how to fill in the new tax return, and what are some of the pitfalls to avoid. There are new powers for automatic penalties, surcharges and interest, and a chapter is devoted to avoiding these. The book also includes a chapter on how to pay less tax. Worked examples and illustrations are included throughout. Don't do your own self assessment before reading this book. John Whiteley FCA is a Chartered Accountant in practice. He has long experience of advising taxpayers in every walk of life. He lives near Exeter in Devon. His daily work involves dealing with the sort of people who would find this book most helpful, (the self-employed, retired people, etc.)

160pp. illus. 1 85703 394 9.

How To Books

How To Books provide practical help on a large range of topics. They are available through all good bookshops or can be ordered direct from the distributors. Just tick the titles you want and complete the form on the following page.

___ Apply to an Industrial Tribunal (£7.99)
___ Applying for a Job (£8.99)
___ Applying for a United States Visa (£15.99)
___ Backpacking Round Europe (£8.99)
___ Be a Freelance Journalist (£8.99)
___ Be a Freelance Secretary (£8.99)
___ Become a Freelance Sales Agent (£9.99)
___ Become an Au Pair (£8.99)
___ Becoming a Father (£8.99)
___ Buy & Run a Shop (£8.99)
___ Buy & Run a Small Hotel (£8.99)
___ Buying a Personal Computer (£9.99)
___ Career Networking (£8.99)
___ Career Planning for Women (£8.99)
___ Cash from your Computer (£9.99)
___ Choosing a Nursing Home (£9.99)
___ Choosing a Package Holiday (£8.99)
___ Claim State Benefits (£9.99)
___ Collecting a Debt (£9.99)
___ Communicate at Work (£7.99)
___ Conduct Staff Appraisals (£7.99)
___ Conducting Effective Interviews (£8.99)
___ Coping with Self Assessment (£9.99)
___ Copyright & Law for Writers (£8.99)
___ Counsel People at Work (£7.99)
___ Creating a Twist in the Tale (£8.99)
___ Creative Writing (£9.99)
___ Critical Thinking for Students (£8.99)
___ Dealing with a Death in the Family (£9.99)
___ Do Voluntary Work Abroad (£8.99)
___ Do Your Own Advertising (£8.99)
___ Do Your Own PR (£8.99)
___ Doing Business Abroad (£10.99)
___ Doing Business on the Internet (£12.99)
___ Emigrate (£9.99)
___ Employ & Manage Staff (£8.99)
___ Find Temporary Work Abroad (£8.99)
___ Finding a Job in Canada (£9.99)
___ Finding a Job in Computers (£8.99)
___ Finding a Job in New Zealand (£9.99)
___ Finding a Job with a Future (£8.99)
___ Finding Work Overseas (£9.99)
___ Freelance DJ-ing (£8.99)
___ Freelance Teaching & Tutoring (£9.99)
___ Get a Job Abroad (£10.99)
___ Get a Job in America (£9.99)
___ Get a Job in Australia (£9.99)
___ Get a Job in Europe (£9.99)
___ Get a Job in France (£9.99)
___ Get a Job in Travel & Tourism (£8.99)
___ Get into Radio (£8.99)
___ Getting into Films & Television (£10.99)

___ Getting That Job (£8.99)
___ Getting your First Job (£8.99)
___ Going to University (£8.99)
___ Helping your Child to Read (£8.99)
___ How to Study & Learn (£8.99)
___ Investing in People (£9.99)
___ Investing in Stocks & Shares (£9.99)
___ Keep Business Accounts (£7.99)
___ Know Your Rights at Work (£8.99)
___ Live & Work in America (£9.99)
___ Live & Work in Australia (£12.99)
___ Live & Work in Germany (£9.99)
___ Live & Work in Greece (£9.99)
___ Live & Work in Italy (£8.99)
___ Live & Work in New Zealand (£9.99)
___ Live & Work in Portugal (£9.99)
___ Live & Work in the Gulf (£9.99)
___ Living & Working in Britain (£8.99)
___ Living & Working in China (£9.99)
___ Living & Working in Hong Kong (£10.99)
___ Living & Working in Israel (£10.99)
___ Living & Working in Saudi Arabia (£12.99)
___ Living & Working in the Netherlands (£9.99)
___ Making a Complaint (£8.99)
___ Making a Wedding Speech (£8.99)
___ Manage a Sales Team (£8.99)
___ Manage an Office (£8.99)
___ Manage Computers at Work (£8.99)
___ Manage People at Work (£8.99)
___ Manage Your Career (£8.99)
___ Managing Budgets & Cash Flows (£9.99)
___ Managing Meetings (£8.99)
___ Managing Your Personal Finances (£8.99)
___ Managing Yourself (£8.99)
___ Market Yourself (£8.99)
___ Master Book-Keeping (£8.99)
___ Mastering Business English (£8.99)
___ Master GCSE Accounts (£8.99)
___ Master Public Speaking (£8.99)
___ Migrating to Canada (£12.99)
___ Obtaining Visas & Work Permits (£9.99)
___ Organising Effective Training (£9.99)
___ Pass Exams Without Anxiety (£7.99)
___ Passing That Interview (£8.99)
___ Plan a Wedding (£8.99)
___ Planning Your Gap Year (£8.99)
___ Prepare a Business Plan (£8.99)
___ Publish a Book (£9.99)
___ Publish a Newsletter (£9.99)
___ Raise Funds & Sponsorship (£7.99)
___ Rent & Buy Property in France (£9.99)
___ Rent & Buy Property in Italy (£9.99)

How To Books

___ Research Methods (£8.99)	___ Use the Internet (£9.99)
___ Retire Abroad (£8.99)	___ Winning Consumer Competitions (£8.99)
___ Return to Work (£7.99)	___ Winning Presentations (£8.99)
___ Run a Voluntary Group (£8.99)	___ Work from Home (£8.99)
___ Setting up Home in Florida (£9.99)	___ Work in an Office (£7.99)
___ Spending a Year Abroad (£8.99)	___ Work in Retail (£8.99)
___ Start a Business from Home (£7.99)	___ Work with Dogs (£8.99)
___ Start a New Career (£6.99)	___ Working Abroad (£14.99)
___ Starting to Manage (£8.99)	___ Working as a Holiday Rep (£9.99)
___ Starting to Write (£8.99)	___ Working in Japan (£10.99)
___ Start Word Processing (£8.99)	___ Working in Photography (£8.99)
___ Start Your Own Business (£8.99)	___ Working in the Gulf (£10.99)
___ Study Abroad (£8.99)	___ Working in Hotels & Catering (£9.99)
___ Study & Live in Britain (£7.99)	___ Working on Contract Worldwide (£9.99)
___ Studying at University (£8.99)	___ Working on Cruise Ships (£9.99)
___ Studying for a Degree (£8.99)	___ Write a Press Release (£9.99)
___ Successful Grandparenting (£8.99)	___ Write a Report (£8.99)
___ Successful Mail Order Marketing (£9.99)	___ Write an Assignment (£8.99)
___ Successful Single Parenting (£8.99)	___ Write & Sell Computer Software (£9.99)
___ Survive Divorce (£8.99)	___ Write for Publication (£8.99)
___ Surviving Redundancy (£8.99)	___ Write for Television (£8.99)
___ Taking in Students (£8.99)	___ Writing a CV that Works (£8.99)
___ Taking on Staff (£8.99)	___ Writing a Non Fiction Book (£9.99)
___ Taking Your A-Levels (£8.99)	___ Writing an Essay (£8.99)
___ Teach Abroad (£8.99)	___ Writing & Publishing Poetry (£9.99)
___ Teach Adults (£8.99)	___ Writing & Selling a Novel (£8.99)
___ Teaching Someone to Drive (£8.99)	___ Writing Business Letters (£8.99)
___ Travel Round the World (£8.99)	___ Writing Reviews (£9.99)
___ Understand Finance at Work (£8.99)	___ Writing Your Dissertation (£8.99)
___ Use a Library (£7.99)	

To: Plymbridge Distributors Ltd, Plymbridge House, Estover Road, Plymouth PL6 7PZ.
Customer Services Tel: (01752) 202301. Fax: (01752) 202331.

Please send me copies of the titles I have indicated. Please add postage & packing (UK £1, Europe including Eire, £2, World £3 airmail).

☐ I enclose cheque/PO payable to Plymbridge Distributors Ltd for £ [＿＿＿＿＿＿＿]

☐ Please charge to my ☐ MasterCard, ☐ Visa, ☐ AMEX card.

Account No. [＿＿＿＿＿＿＿＿＿＿＿＿＿＿＿＿＿]

Card Expiry Date [＿＿] 19 ☎ **Credit Card orders may be faxed or phoned.**

Customer Name (CAPITALS) ....

Address ....

.... Postcode ....

Telephone........................... Signature ....

Every effort will be made to despatch your copy as soon as possible but to avoid possible disappointment please allow up to 21 days for despatch time (42 days if overseas). Prices and availability are subject to change without notice.

[Code BPA]